Studying Urban
Youth Culture
PRIMER

PETER LANG
New York • Washington, D.C./Baltimore • Bern
Frankfurt am Main • Berlin • Brussels • Vienna • Oxford

Greg Dimitriadis

Studying Urban
Youth Culture

PRIMER

PETER LANG
New York • Washington, D.C./Baltimore • Bern
Frankfurt am Main • Berlin • Brussels • Vienna • Oxford

Library of Congress Cataloging-in-Publication Data

Dimitriadis, Greg.
Studying urban youth culture primer / Greg Dimitriadis.
p. cm.
Includes bibliographical references.
1. Urban youth—United States. I. Title.
HQ796.D484   305.23509173'20973—dc22   2007042504
ISBN 978-0-8204-7269-0

Bibliographic information published by **Die Deutsche Nationalbibliothek**.
Die Deutsche Nationalbibliothek lists this publication in the "Deutsche
Nationalbibliografie"; detailed bibliographic data are available
on the Internet at http://dnb.d-nb.de/.

Cover design by Clear Point Designs

© 2008 Peter Lang Publishing, Inc., New York
29 Broadway, 18th floor, New York, NY 10006
www.peterlang.com

Printed in the United States of America

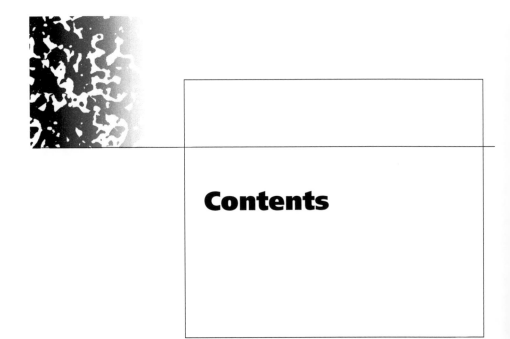

Contents

Acknowledgments

I thank Kathleen Nolan and Lois Weis for their close readings of this book in draft form. Kathleen provided excellent commentary on the historical texts and critical concepts I was using, forcing me to clarify them and make them more nuanced at key points. Lois pushed me (as she has over the years) on several important issues, including gender, new methodological presses for qualitative inquiry, and the role of the IRB. She also suggested key, organizational changes which (I hope) will make the text clearer and more readable. We also coauthored (as noted) key parts of this book. Thanks to them both. Thanks, as well, to Kristin Cipollone and Bernadette Shade. Thanks also to Joe Kincheloe and Shirley Steinberg for inviting me to contribute this volume and to Chris Myers for never giving up on it!

A Brief Note

Studying Urban Youth Culture Primer is an incomplete
and partial text. It represents my own short "take"
on an emergent field that works across several different disciplines—sociology, anthropology, communication, and education, among them. As I note
throughout, it is an often intensely problematic field
of inquiry—in particular, it is a field often marked
by the "**othering**" of so-called urban youth, a term
that has typically come to stand in for or represent
a whole host of racialized social pathologies. In fact,
"urban youth" itself has emerged as a marketing
category, intimately linked to hip-hop culture and
used to sell products to young people around the
world. In this text, I look to both interrogate these
discourses and suggest ways we can move beyond
them. This is a text that aims for a theoretical, historical, and methodological intervention—all in less
than 50,000 words. I will inevitably leave out some
key texts and ideas and perhaps overstate the importance of others. This is, again, an incomplete and
partial text—but hopefully a useful one.

Othering

process by which a group or
individual is marked as
fundamentally different from
what is perceived to be
normal or mainstream.

GLOSSARY

Othering—process by which a group or individual is marked as fundamentally different from what is perceived to be normal or mainstream.

CHAPTER ONE

Introduction

Studying Urban Youth Culture. Each word evokes a rich, historically complex, and sometimes contradictory set of meanings. As a whole, the phrase is remarkably elastic and polysemantic, taking us to various substantive terrains, with all manner of interpretive lenses. In the early part of the twentieth century, the notion of "studying urban youth culture" would evoke Chicago School sociologists such as Frederick Thrasher, Robert Park, Louis Wirth, and others, all of whom looked at different neighborhoods in Chicago as discrete "laboratories" for the growth and (sometimes) assimilation of new immigrants. Thrasher's magisterial *The Gang: A Study of 1,313 Gangs in Chicago* (taken up in more detail in the next chapter) would stand as perhaps the earliest, most complete testament to this impulse. Today, studying urban youth culture might not be tied so closely to particular notions of place. The isomorphic relationship between place and culture has been called inextricably into question, as "urban" cultural products such as hip-hop "flow" across national borders and boundaries in new and intensified ways. "Urban" no longer can so easily be located, either geographically or symbolically. Today, a study of "urban youth culture" might very well be a study of "a close knit circle of housewives in the suburbs of Cleveland, all in their late twenties and early thirties," planning a trip to see a sold-out Eminem concert in Detroit (Kitwana, 2005, p. 5). Or a study of restless Arab youths in the outskirts of Paris narrating their frustrations through indigenous French rap while prophesying the riots of late 2005 (much as their counterparts did more than a decade earlier in Los Angeles). "Studying urban youth culture" is thus a complex affair, both theoretically and methodologically. In this introduction, I pull apart each of these terms before drawing them back together. In doing so, I look toward a new language for working with and understanding the experiences of marginalized youths in the United States and around the world today.

Studying

Quantitative research measures the statistical relationship between discrete variables, often positing "causal" or "associative" relationships between them.

Qualitative research creates "ground-up" understandings of specific phenomena, particularly from the point of view of research participants. Data collection techniques include open-ended interviews, observations, participant-observations, and various kinds of document analysis.

Social scientific research is often divided into two "camps"—quantitative and qualitative. **Quantitative research** is typically concerned with measuring the statistical relationship between discrete variables, often positing causal or associative relationships between them. So, for example, a quantitative approach to studying urban youths might look at the relationship between risk factors and gang involvement (e.g., Thornberry, 1998). **Qualitative research** is typically concerned with creating ground-up understandings of particular phenomena, especially from the point of view of research participants. Qualitative researchers use a range of data collection techniques, including open-ended interviews, observations, participant-observations, and various document analysis techniques (detailed in Chapter 5). The goal is to understand phenomena in their naturalistic contexts. A qualitative approach to studying urban youths might look at the complex, multifaceted experiences of a small handful of youths over time and place, as in Mark Fleisher's *Dead End Kids: Gang Girls and the Boys They Know* (1998) or my own *Friendship, Cliques, and Gangs: Young Black Men Coming of Age in Urban America* (2003).

This volume concentrates on the latter approach, qualitative research, as it has traditionally been used to give us rich understandings of young people's cultural lives. Yet it is important to note that these two research approaches need not be seen as mutually exclusive. In particular, it is important to resist the notion that quantitative research is "conservative" in its orientation, whereas qualitative research is more "progressive." Each type of research allows us to see certain things we might not see otherwise. What is true, however, is that qualitative research gives us more opportunities to connect with and involve ourselves in the lives of the people with whom we work. This does not necessarily mean that such work is more humane or politically progressive by nature—it is often quite the opposite.

In fact, the term "studying" itself evokes a kind of clinical, taxonomic impulse that has been closely linked to imperialist projects. One typically "studies" those with less power. Indeed, the entire history of the social sciences can be said to be a history of the powerful studying the less powerful for other powerful people. As Vidich and Lyman note (2000), the earliest efforts at ethnography were conducted by missionaries and other colonists who looked to understand the lives of "other" groups around the world, assumed to be primitive. **Ethnography** is a methodological approach that looks to describe in depth and with detail the social practices of groups or individuals. Although the term is often used quite loosely to describe any qualitative project, the gold standard for such work typically consists of long-term engagement (at least a year), as well as multiple forms of data. The earliest such work, as noted, treated various "others" as exotic, premodern cultures. The goal for missionaries and other colonizers was to understand how "earlier" forms of

Ethnography
a methodological approach that looks to describe in depth and detail the social practices of groups or individuals.

culture—typically, pre-Christian—exist in contemporary time.

In many respects, the disciplines of anthropology and sociology were both rooted in this impulse. Each looked to understand exotic others. For anthropology in the United States, this meant a study of Native Americans, as well as an interest in non-Western cultures around the world. For sociology in the United States, this meant a study of various immigrant groups, particularly in Chicago. A normative impulse marked these efforts, as it did for researchers around the world (for example, in Britain where there has been a strong tradition of ethnographic work). Although the goal was often a purported cultural comparison, invariably this work created sharp cultural hierarchies. This often meant, to echo Michelle Fine, stark splits between "self" and "other"—a distinction which has marked the entire history of this work. According to Fine, this history has been marked by "textual laminations within which Others have been sealed by social scientists." She continues, there has been a "complicity of researchers in the construction and distancing of Others" (1994, p. 71).

This distancing has been challenged by many over the past twenty years. Much of this work began when anthropologists James Clifford and George Marcus (1986) called into question the project of **"writing culture."** According to Clifford and Marcus, anthropological texts were created by authors, often deploying the rhetorical techniques of fiction, and could thus be seen largely as interpretive and not scientific endeavors. This led to a wide-ranging paralysis in the field. That is, with all such work seemingly reduced to the status of fiction, many felt ethnographic work no longer had a clear point or mission. These new challenges to "studying others" led to a range of responses. One such response—one I want to take up here and in the next chapter—is an increased reflexivity about our multiple roles in the field and at the desk. To echo Michelle Fine (1994), field workers today must

Writing culture
the realization that anthropological texts were created by authors often deploying the rhetorical techniques of fiction and could thus be seen largely as interpretive and not scientific endeavors.

"work the hyphen" in their different roles (e.g., participant-observer), always acknowledging the roles they inhabit, including what they allow and what they deny. Indeed, according to Fine, researchers must actively work against "othering" in field work, objectively creating neatly bounded subjects on which to report, while they must also resist self-reflexivity or navel gazing, the danger of looking inward as a way to avoid the ethical responsibility of acting in the world. More recently, Fine and Weis (1998) have extended these concerns to explicitly address the complexities of political activism and policymaking. They argue, in *The Unknown City*, that we must try to "meld *writing about* and *working with*" politically invested actors in more compelling and constitutive ways (p. 277). Ultimately, they call us to "think through the power, obligations, and responsibilities of social research" on multiple levels, accounting for multiple social contexts and concerns (Fine, Weis, Weseen, and Wong, 2000, p. 108). These concerns have been taken up recently by those conducting youth participatory action research (YPAR)—research conducted with young people (not on them) around the issues they find most pressing in their lives. Such work looks to "illuminate how youth agency contributes to more vibrant and inclusive democracy and informed public policy" (Ginwright and Cammarota, 2006, p. xvi). This, too, will be taken up in more detail later.

This is a great challenge for those of us "studying urban youth culture." How do we avoid creating debilitating "fictions" about the "other?" How can we more ethically work with others? This means pulling apart two terms that have been used to "laminate" others in neat fictions such as "urban" and "youth." Each will be discussed in turn.

Urban

The term "urban" is both geographic and symbolic. Traditionally, urban areas have been marked by high densities and concentrations of people, particularly

Urban

both "densely settled"
territories and a term with a
symbolic resonance, often
(and often negatively)
associated with the lives and
experiences of working-class
African Americans.

in relation to suburban and rural areas. The 2000 U.S. Census defines "**urban**" areas as "densely settled" territories that consist of "core census block groups or blocks that have a population density of at least 1,000 people per square mile" and "surrounding census blocks that have an overall density of at least 500 people per square mile." As I discuss in the next chapter, such spaces have captured the imaginations of social scientists for several decades. The earliest sociologists saw "the city" as a laboratory where different immigrant ethnic groups came and seemingly worked toward assimilating themselves into "mainstream" American culture. The earliest studies looked at the social and spatial organization of urban centers as ethnic enclaves—including Jewish, Italian, and Polish ones. Recall here the pioneering work of sociologist Robert Park. In his classic 1925 essay, "The City: Suggestions for the Investigation of Human Behavior in the Urban Environment," Park discusses the ways in which cities are more than "a congeries of individual men and of social conveniences—streets, buildings, electric lights, tramways, and telephones, etc." They were also more than "a mere constellation of institutions and administrative devices—courts, hospitals, schools, police, and civil functionaries." He continues, "The city is, rather, a state of mind, a body of customs and traditions, and of the organized attitudes and sentiments that inhere in these customs and are transmitted with this tradition" (p. x).

For Park and others, the city provided rich material for study, particularly near the turn of the century, with massive influxes of immigrants into the United States, many of whom congregated and concentrated in areas such as Chicago. We see much of that fascination in this early work. As Park notes, the discipline of anthropology had long been concerned with the lives and experiences of so-called primitive people. These same methods might be applied to cities. He notes,

> The same patient methods of observation which anthropologists like Boas and Lowie have expended

on the study of the life and manners of the North American Indian might be even more fruitfully employed in the investigation of the customs, beliefs, social practices, and general conceptions of life prevalent in Little Italy on the lower North Side in Chicago, or in recording the more sophisticated folkways of the inhabitants of Greenwich Village and the neighborhood of Washington Square, New York. (p. 3)

We see a kind of fascination with the "other" here. This meant, for the earliest sociologists, a study of poor, ethnic enclaves. For example, William Foote Whyte's *Street Corner Society: The Social Structure of an Italian Slum* (1943/1993) was a look at Italian immigrants in Boston. Taken up in more detail in the next chapter, this was a story of two different young men—Chick and Doc and their social networks. These were, respectively, the "college boys" and the "corner boys." As Whyte makes clear, each had a different attitude toward assimilating into mainstream American culture. Chick worked through the mainstream, socially prescribed channels. Doc, on the other hand, held on more tightly to his Italian identity and the notions of extended kinship they implied. Where Chick came to separate himself from the group and to hold tight to a particular form of individualism, Doc's identity was much more tied to the local group. Where Chick looked to move out of the neighborhood, Doc stayed close to his roots. In many respects, Whyte looked to establish the autonomy and order of what he called a "slum."

As in much of the work that would follow, however, Whyte worked to "other" these urban residents. The city was an illicit, dangerous place filled with new and different ethnic groups. Working against the tide of pathologizing discourses about ethnic others, these studies helped to proliferate these discourses as well. Published in 1943, *Street Corner Society* crystallized this particular research ethic. By the mid-1960s, discourses about urban centers had moved away from a focus on "ethnic others" such as Italians to racial others—in particular, African Americans. This reflects of course a broader shift in the ways in which "difference" was understood in the United States. By the 1960s, notions of "the urban" took on a distinctly racial overtone. We see this dynamic in the studies that emerged during this period—*Soulside: Inquiries in Ghetto Culture and Community* (1969) by Ulf Hannerz and *Tally's Corner: A Study of Negro Streetcorner Men* (1967) by Eliot Liebow. Like earlier studies, these studies looked to highlight the logic inherent in so-called ghettos, now inextricably linked to poor African Americans, and largely focused on men.

For example, *Soulside* looks closely at notions of "ghetto-specific masculinity" and how these helped to constitute a "ghetto-specific complex" that served as a seemingly stark contrast to the mainstream American culture. He sums up, "Among the components of this ghetto-specific complex are for instance female household dominance; a ghetto-specific male role of somewhat varying expression including, among other emphases, a toughness, sexual activity, and a fair amount of liquor consumption; a relatively conflict-ridden relationship between the sexes," and so on (1969, p. 177). As Duneier (1992) argues, these would largely be the "stereotypes" that would plague black men in both the popular and academic literature. They would provide a certain notion of black maleness that would come to stand in for the "whole" of so-called ghetto culture, further perpetrating notions that the "urban" was a largely exotic, distant culture within the U.S. environs. The picture was not particularly flattering—that of tough-talking men who didn't work, drank, used women for sex, and spent their days on street corners.

In many respects, these cultural portraits were written by well-meaning white men who looked to contest the often more explicitly racist discourses circulating at the time and open up important questions about poverty. They often looked to create a kind of cultural cohesion often assumed to be missing by dominant American approaches. These studies were extended by sociologists including William Julius Wilson and Elijah Anderson, who argued that this culture was a response to the steady decline of the economic infrastructure that left urban areas with fewer and fewer positive role models who could help youth in these "ghettos" connect with those outside. From the middle of the twentieth century, with the rapid ascent of deindustrialization, jobs began to disappear from urban centers, leaving behind those who, in effect, had no other options. This led to what Wilson (1996) called a "ghetto-related" set of behaviors that are largely self-destructive and self-perpetuating and that do not lead to gainful employment outside of rapidly deteriorating urban centers.

Although Wilson locates these issues in broader economic and structural inequalities, he too works largely to perpetuate notions that a pathological set of behaviors are "transmitted" in urban centers. As Cameron McCarthy (1998) notes, such notions of "the urban" are reinforced in popular culture—through films such as *Menace II Society* and *Boyz N the Hood,* as well as hip-hop culture more broadly. A particular "code of the real" operates in these popular culture forms, a code that works to create notions of "the inner city" as distinct from suburban ones—locating in the former a whole host of problems seen as endemic to these centers and their inhabitants. "The urban" has come to symbolize a range of social ills and uncertainties in this self-perpetuating dichotomy, most often outside of broader structural analysis.

Indeed, "urban" is itself a highly contested term. Although it has come to symbolize a kind of racial codeword for pathology, it is also the terrain upon which the most significant and important youth culture movement of the late-twentieth century was born—**hip-hop**. As Jeff Chang (2005), Tricia Rose (1994), and Murray Forman (2002) have argued, the so-called urban renewal projects of the 1970s worked to further isolate black and other poor and minority populations. The paradigmatic case here is the Cross

---

Hip-hop

often associated with rap music alone, hip-hop was a cultural response to wide-scale social dislocation of urban areas in the mid-1970s that encompassed rap music, DJing, break dancing, and graffiti writing.

Bronx Expressway built in the 1960s, which worked
to tear apart and disrupt well-functioning neighborhoods in the South Bronx, leaving in its wake pock-
ets of urban blight, and a vicious downward spiral
of poverty and violence. Hip-hop was born out of
this destruction. It was a cultural response that
drew together rap music, DJing, break dancing, and
graffiti writing—a cultural nexus that has largely
defined global youth culture as it moved around
the United States and eventually around the world.
In fact, many of the most salacious aspects of so-
called urban culture have been sold by African
American youth themselves to consumers around
the world in complex and often problematic ways.
These representations have, of course, been the
subject of much public debate and dialogue. What
is clear is that "the urban" remains a site of fascination and danger today as it did for the earliest
Chicago School sociologists.

Finally, it is impossible to discuss "the urban"
today without discussing the ways in which "global
cities" are increasingly interconnected, often in
unpredictable ways. With the increasingly global
flows of people, monies, images, technologies, and
ideas, cities are highly contested and often paradoxical places. For example, new flows of wealth
have created enormous economic disparity in city
centers, with the ultrarich and the massively poor
living side by side. Cities are marked by new immigrant groups creating ethnic, racial, and religious
enclaves in cities such as Toronto, London, and New
York City, which often force heretofore unimagined
kinds of cultural conflicts, dialogues, and syner-
gies. How we represent cities today is very much
an open question, with many resorting to flexible,
aesthetic forms such as the novel. One recalls here
the massively popular *White Teeth* by Zadie Smith
(2000). Yet it is important to remember that the
earliest sociologists recognized the power of the literary in representing the complexities and nuances
of city life. As Robert Park wrote in 1925, "We are
mainly indebted to writers of fiction for our more

intimate knowledge of contemporary urban life. But the life of our cities demands a more searching and disinterested study" (1925, p. 3). Indeed, the discipline of sociology itself was part of this effort to build a more searching and disinterested way of understanding city life.

Youth

Youth

a highly contested category, often used to refer to minors (those under the age of 18). The notion of "youth" is historically constructed, often linked to the emergence during the early to mid-twentieth century of popular culture forms such as rock and roll. It is a category that can have profoundly different meanings across culture and class.

Youth is a highly contested term—historically evolving, often assumed to be stable, and deployed in a range of ways with concrete effects for the most vulnerable populations. Indeed, as Gary Cross asked in his recent book *The Cute and the Cool* (2004), "a fifteen-year-old boy having sex with a female teacher is a victim, whereas the ten-year-old killer is a criminal. The former is a child; the latter is not. Does this make sense?" (p. 11). Of course, it does not. But the question does in fact evoke the confusion many experience around "youth" as a category—a category that evokes both timeless and transcendent innocence as well as deep-rooted fears and anxieties, often at the same time.

The term "youth" is a relatively recent invention. As Steinberg and Kincheloe (2004), among others, have made clear, the notion of "youth" as a protected and privileged "in-between" stage was largely generated over the course of the twentieth century. On one level, this notion of youth emerged as part of a broader discourse about the scientific management of children and their "healthy development"—a movement headed up by a new class of "child-reading experts" (Cross, 2004, p. 35). On another, this notion of youth was co-constituted through its growth as a commercial marketing category. We see this, for example, in the rise of fantasy and adventure entertainment beginning in the late 1930s targeted toward youths themselves (and not their parents). Cross writes, "In the new world of the comic book, movie serial, and radio program, the child could choose his (or her) own forms of fantasy, not merely accept the parents' nostalgic version of play" (p. 142). In fact, the rise of fantasy

Moral panics
widespread or even epidemic
cultural panics around
specific subcultural practices
or other cultural forms, often
linked to seemingly deviant
groups.

and adventure entertainment led to one of the first large-scale **"moral panics"** around youths—Frederick Wertham's book *Seduction of the Innocent,* which led to congressional hearings on comic book culture. According to Wertham, comic books were leading young people down a path of delinquency and were responsible for many of the psychological problems young people had. The testimony led, famously, to the imposition of the "comics code"—a set of guidelines for what could and could not appear in comics. Such moral panics have regularly emerged in response to new forms of youth culture and entertainment—from comic books in the mid-twentieth century to the videogames of the early twenty-first century.

Youth culture crystallized in many ways during the mid-1950s and early 1960s with the rise of rock and roll as well as a host of other cultural products aimed at teenagers. Indeed, it was during this period that the teenage years became constructed firmly as a protected and privileged in-between stage—one distinct from childhood and adulthood. "Youth culture" became years where one could delay the onset of adulthood, could try on and put off different identities before entering into a seemingly solidified adult persona. Rock and roll, however, led to another moral panic—the notion that this music was corrupting young people, a fear linked inextricably to the racialized body. Most famously, Elvis Presley's gyrating hips were seen as profound dangers to youths, representing a kind of sexuality associated with African Americans. The particular notion of "youth" that emerged in these years was largely marked as "white" and middle class.

Social psychologists have picked up similar such notions of youth as timeless and universal, describing "adolescence" as a time when young people struggle to define themselves by trying on different identities. This notion of adolescence, as Wyn and White (1997) point out, "assumes a 'pre-social' self . . . which exists within the individual but which must be found and developed ('finding one's self').

The individual is seen as distinct from and separate from society, as possessing a 'self' independent from social relationships or social circumstances" (p. 53). On this logic, moving from adolescence to adulthood means moving from a state of dependency to one of independence and autonomy. This is the privileged model of **adolescent development**. In particular, reaching adulthood means separating one's self (materially and otherwise) from one's family and parents.

Such notions, however, often do not map easily onto the lives, experiences, and needs of many disenfranchised youths—particularly youths of color. For many disenfranchised youths, adolescence is an ambiguous life stage with competing "role expectations" and mixed messages about "successful" development (Burton, Obeidallah, and Allison, 1996, p. 120). Middle-class norms about distinct life stages and clear transitions do not wholly apply here. Perhaps most important, everyday material demands often bring the worlds of parents and children together in ways that belie a neat separation between the two. For example, middle-class adolescents and adults have traditionally used income level and job status to mark generation distinctions. However, many marginalized youths work side by side with their parents in service sector "McJobs"— often the only available work for people without advanced degrees—and must contribute all or part of that income to household maintenance (p. 130). Clear lines and demarcations between those older and younger generations are often blurred or simply nonexistent, raising a series of key problematics. We must, therefore, work against notions of youth that reify its assumed "whiteness" and "middle-class" status. We must do so, however, without reifying a competing "minority" or "working-class" version. Studying youth puts us squarely in the middle of such tensions.

Although "youth" has been constructed as timeless and immutable in the popular and academic imagination, it has remained a site of profound

---

Adolescent development
the pathway young people take from their preteen years to early adulthood.

ambivalence and fear. In particular, many critical theorists, including those in cultural studies,
argue that the notion of youth itself is now being
assaulted by our consumer culture, which has targeted youths with an increasing amount of information and resources. Young people are largely, to
evoke Joe Kincheloe, left "home alone" with popular culture to raise them. Our so-called postmodern
children are facing a media saturation that is also
working to blur the lines between adolescence and
adulthood. As Kincheloe (1998) notes,

> In the postmodern childhood, being home alone
> is an everyday reality. Children now know what
> only adults used to know: postmodern children
> are sexually knowledgeable and often sexually
> experienced; they understand and may have
> experimented with drugs and alcohol; and new
> studies show they often experience the same pres-
> sures as single working mothers, as they manage
> the stresses of school, work at home, and interper-
> sonal family dynamics. (p. 171)

Here, too, notions of adolescence as a clear developmental stage have been called into question.

All of this underscores the ways "youth" has
become an ambivalent category, one that adults
seemingly need to protect, though one which adults
are abandoning and reviling in equal measure.
Something like a "war on youth," to echo Henry
Giroux (2004), is being conducted on young people
today. As the public sphere continues to erode, we
see less and less of an investment in young people as
the future. We see this, as Giroux, Grossberg (2005),
Males (1996), and others have pointed out, in the
appalling levels of poverty and "nonspectacular"
violence young people face. Indeed, as Grossberg
points out, young people today face unprecedented
levels of poverty and violence. In the face of a growing discourse on "family values," Grossberg writes,
33 percent of children will live in poverty at some
point in their childhood years; 25 percent are born
poor; and 20 percent are currently living in poverty.
Young people are the fastest growing and largest
percentage of the homeless in the United States,

with an average age of nine years old. The figures are markedly worse than for other countries such as Canada and Sweden. In addition, young people are facing unprecedented levels of violence. As is well known by now, the United States has a higher level of infant mortality than any other country in the industrial world. Moreover, 75 percent of all violent deaths among youths in the industrialized world occur in the United States. And this is not youth-on-youth crime. One out of every three such violent deaths is caused by an adult.

The figures go on and on. As Grossberg (2005) so aptly puts it, we live in a "child-hating world" (p. 351). Indeed, the public discourse on young people is largely a punitive one. As public services are increasingly cut, we have an exploding prison system that incarcerates more and more youths. If young people used to "learn to labor," they now "learn to do time" (Nolan and Anyon, 2004). The public response around youth is largely adult driven, largely ambivalent (at best) and mean spirited (at worse). No one has felt the brunt of neoliberalism, the withering of the public sphere, or the rise of rampant worldwide capitalist logics more than young people.

To repeat, "youth" is a contested term. It is a term that has largely been naturalized through developmental and commercial discourses as a privileged in-between stage. Yet it is a term that hides a host of complexities, ambivalences, and hostilities, generated largely by adults. Meeting young people "where they're at" demands looking at this term critically. It demands a sensitivity to the ways young people live their lives. This takes us to the terrain of culture.

Culture

an extraordinarily complex term that often refers to "high culture" (literature, art, music, philosophy, and the like). This very elitist notion of culture exists side by side with another notion of culture—that of a "whole way of life."

Culture

As cultural studies scholar Raymond Williams (1961) so famously noted, "**culture**" is "one of the two or three most complicated words in the English language." As he notes, the word has historically been linked to the notion of high culture, the so-called crowning achievements of particular civilizations—their literature, art, music, philosophy, and so forth. High culture has historically been the purview of the upper classes. Indeed, part of maintaining elite status is aligning oneself with these cultural forms—a point Bourdieu (1984) underscores in *Distinction*. This very elitist notion of culture exists side by side with another notion of culture—that of a "whole way of life." Culture, here, can be located in the everyday social interplay among the range of artifacts, ideas, and institutions people produce and live through. The cultural forms examined here need not be ones marked as elite or distinct; they can be everyday artifacts, such as popular music, television shows, movies, fashion, and food. These cultural forms can tell us much about how particular groups of people understand themselves and others. The relationship between "textual" and "lived" culture has been an abiding concern of **cultural studies**—the interdisciplinary study of "culture," particularly how it is lived in the quotidian. These concerns will be taken up in detail in the following chapter.

Cultural Studies
an interdisciplinary area of inquiry often associated with scholars at Birmingham University, largely a response to theories that reduced all cultural practices to an extension of the economy. Scholars in cultural studies look at the work and autonomy of culture.

For now, it is important to highlight and point out all the ways in which the notion of "culture" itself has changed in the ethnographic imagination over time. As Rosaldo (1990) points out, the earliest iterations of culture in anthropology were rooted in a colonial impulse to control "'distant' peoples and places" (p. 30). These notions of culture tended to focus on the broad patterns and commonalities that seemingly inhered in particular cultures. The goal was not to understand culture as emergent and unfolding; it was to "capture" culture as a timeless and immutable—a frozen snapshot in time. Of course, this worked to create sharp and debilitating dichotomies between "self" and "other" in the literature about non-Western cultures. "We" typically exist in the present—emergent, unfolding, heterogeneous, and unpredictable. "They" typically exist as a relic of the past—unchanging, static, homogeneous, and predictable. "They" are akin to museum pieces, according to Rosaldo, underscoring the "objectivist" and "monumentalist" discourses that bind them.

These notions of culture implied stark splits between researchers and subjects, as noted above. They implied, as well, that individual informants could speak for entire cultures, their norms, beliefs, and so on. In this sense, members of a particular culture were seen as largely interchangeable and commensurable with one another. This is, of course, a function of power. Members of dominant groups are seen as individuals, with complex biographies. Members of subordinate groups are seen as extensions of collectives, members of a group. This production of beliefs and knowledge about "the other" was termed "**Orientalism**" by Edward Said. Orientalism is an exploration of the ways in which Western scholars have produced a mutually reinforcing distinction between "the Orient" and "the Occident" to understand the Middle East. For Said, Orientalism is a "corporate institution for dealing with the Orient—dealing with it by making statements about it, authorizing views of it, describing it, by teaching it, settling it, ruling over it: in short, Orientalism as a Western style for dominating, restructuring, and having authority over the Orient" (1978/2003, p. 3). Much of this, for Said, is about the production of a self-reinforcing and propelling field of knowledge and inquiry—the production of expertise and authority about the Orient and the Occident.

Such notions of "culture" have come in for critique on several different fronts. Much of this critique originated and unfolded with the work of anthropologist Clifford Geertz. His landmark book *The Interpretation of Cultures* (1973) represented a turning point for anthropology. Here, Geertz argued that culture was "semiotic," that "man is an animal suspended in webs of significance he himself has spun."(p. 5). The study of culture was, in essence, the study of those webs. For Geertz, reading cultures is like reading texts—the analysis of culture is "therefore not an experimental science in search

Orientalism

an exploration of the ways in which Western scholars have produced a mutually reinforcing distinction between "the Orient" and "the Occident" to understand the Middle East.

of law but an interpretive one in search of meaning" (p. 5). From this perspective, anthropology is the construction of other people's constructions of their realities. Geertz signaled an interpretive turn in anthropology. He argued that cultures were not "out there" to be objectively captured through neutral forms of representation. Instead, cultures are always already the product of interpretive work. Individuals are meaning-making agents in context; this includes research subjects and participants as well as the ethnographers who study them. Geertz's contributions have been many, including his new and complex ways to think about the nature of culture. According to anthropologist Sherry Ortner (1999), Geertz offers a notion of culture that bridges the social scientific and the humanistic. He makes us think of culture "as the clash of meanings in the borderlands; as public culture that has its own textual coherence but is always locally interpreted; as fragile webs of meaning woven by vulnerable actors in nightmarish situations; as the grounds of agency and intentionality in ongoing practice" (p. 11).

Geertz's notion of culture was critical to the so-called crisis of representation which became pronounced in anthropology in the mid-1980s, particularly with the work of James Clifford and George Marcus and the volume *Writing Culture* (1986). In opening up a discussion about the textual nature of culture and the interpretive nature of inquiry, Geertz underscored a key insight of this move—that writing is not epiphenomenal to but constitutive of the research process itself. In the introduction to *Writing Culture,* James Clifford wrote, "We begin, not with participant-observation or with cultural texts . . . but with writing, the making of texts. No longer a marginal, or occulted, dimension, writing has emerged as central to what we do both in the field and thereafter."(p. 2). He went on to note, "The fact that it has not until recently been portrayed or seriously discussed reflects the persistence of an ideology claiming transparency of representation and immediacy of experience" (p. 2). Different genres of writing and different semiotic media (writing, photography, video) afford different kinds of access to experience and the world. Challenges to viewing writing (and other semiotic forms) uncritically as representational (and not performative and productive) led to critiques of anthropological work conducted by anthropologists in earlier times, such as those highlighted by Edward Said.

The next generation of researchers looked to move beyond the "paralysis" associated with the "writing culture" movement—looked to understand, describe, and explain culture, but in "noninnocent" ways. To return to the work of Rosaldo, many now see culture in a different way, as a flow of goods and products across national borders and boundaries. We live in a moment of "**globalization**"—a term referring to the broad range of material, cultural, and technological shifts and dislocations that have marked the past several decades. Here, semiotic forms travel across the world in new and complex ways through a plethora of information technologies. According to Rosaldo, the old "monumentalist" model suggests an art museum, with distinct pieces available for and on view. We need to reconceptualize this as something closer to a "garage sale," he notes, "a precise image for the postcolonial situation where cultural artifacts flow between unlikely places, and nothing is sacred, permanent, or sealed off" (1990, p. 44). This version of "culture" demands a different research imaginary, one that looks beyond individual, discrete sites and settings. This is the subject of Chapter 3.

In sum, culture remains a vital, lived category, but one that cannot be seen as timeless and immutable. In many respects, this takes us to the terrain of method—a set of concerns taken up in detail in Chapter 5.

Globalization

the broad range of material, cultural, and technological shifts and dislocations that have marked the past several decades. The term is often used to highlight new, massive concentrations of wealth, as well as the new ways in which popular, cultural texts are circulating around the world in complex and unpredictable ways.

Studying Urban Youth Culture

Studying urban youth culture is a complex affair. As we pull these terms apart, we need to put them back together, to put them to work. The charge is a complex one—one that several recent studies have taken on (Brotherton and Barrios, 2004; Dance, 2002; Jackson, 2001; Nolan, 2007; Vargas, 2006; among others to be discussed in detail later). Understanding the complicated, discursive history of these terms forces us to see that they are all "dangerous" in one way or another. There are no safe spaces. Opening ourselves up to this kind of reflexivity forces us to think through the terrain outlined above at every turn as we move forward with our projects. In particular, we must face the often dominating histories of sociology, as well as the meta-field(s) of qualitative inquiry more broadly. These methodological techniques have often been used to "other" marginalized youths, to calcify their lives and experiences in debilitating and destructive ways. We must engage the lives and cultures of these youths in this light, in new and hopefully more ethical ways. Moving across the fields of sociology, anthropology, education, and beyond, this short text may help us to think through this terrain in more nuanced ways. We now examine these histories in depth.

GLOSSARY

Adolescent development—term taken from psychology describing the pathway young people take from their preteen years to early adulthood. This term typically privileges a model of adolescence that assumes it an "in between" time, when young people can try different identities on and off. Adolescent development is largely a middle-class concept.

Cultural Studies—an interdisciplinary area of inquiry often associated with scholars at Birmingham University in the United Kingdom, including Stuart Hall, Raymond Williams, E. P. Thompson, and Richard Hoggart. Cultural studies was largely a response to theories that reduced all cultural practices to an extension of the economy. Scholars in cultural studies look at the work and autonomy of culture. Such scholars have tended to be concerned with popular culture as well as the quotidian lives of working-class youths.

Culture—an extraordinarily complex term that often refers to "high culture," the so-called crowning achievements of particular civilizations—their literature, art, music, philosophy, and the like. High culture has historically been the purview of the upper classes. This very elitist notion of culture exists side by side with another notion of culture—that of a "whole way of life." Culture, here, can be located in the everyday social interplay between the range of artifacts, ideas, and institutions people produce and live through.

Ethnography—a methodological approach that looks to describe in depth and detail the social practices of groups or individuals. Although the term is often used quite loosely to describe any qualitative project, the "gold standard" for such work typically consists of a long-term engagement (at least a year), as well as multiple forms of data.

Globalization—the broad range of material, cultural, and technological shifts and dislocations that have marked the past several decades. The term is often used to highlight new, massive concentrations of wealth, as well as the new ways in which popular, cultural texts are circulating around the world in complex and unpredictable ways.

Hip-hop—often associated with rap music alone, hip-hop was a cultural response to wide-scale social dislocation of urban areas in the mid-1970s that encompassed rap music, DJing, break dancing, and graffiti writing. This cultural nexus has largely defined global youth culture as it moved around the United States and eventually around the world.

Moral panics—widespread or even epidemic cultural panics around specific subcultural practices or other cultural forms, often linked to seemingly deviant groups. One of the earliest moral panics was around deviancy and comic books. More recently, we have seen moral panics around hip-hop music and videogames.

Orientalism—an exploration of the ways in which Western scholars have produced a mutually reinforcing distinction between "the Orient" and "the Occident" to understand the Middle East. For Edward Said (with whom the term is typically associated), Orientalism is a "corporate institution for dealing with the Orient—dealing with it by making statements about it, authorizing views of it, describing it, by teaching it, settling it, ruling over it: in short, Orientalism as a Western style for dominating, restructuring, and having authority over the Orient" (1978/1993, p. 3).

Qualitative research—an approach to research typically concerned with creating "ground-up" understandings of particular phenomena, particularly from the point of view of research participants. Qualitative researchers use a range of data collection techniques, including open-ended interviews, observations, participant-observations, and various kinds of document analysis techniques.

Quantitative research—an approach to research typically concerned with measuring the statistical relationship between discrete variables, often positing "causal" or "associative" relationships between them.

Urban—the 2000 U.S. Census defines "urban" areas as "densely settled" territories that consist of "core census block groups or blocks that have a population density of at least 1,000 people per square mile" and "surrounding census blocks that have an overall density of at least 500 people per square mile." The "urban" also has a symbolic resonance, often (and often negatively) associated with the lives and experiences of working-class African Americans.

Writing culture—associated with the work of James Clifford and George Marcus; the realization that anthropological texts were created by authors often deploying the rhetorical techniques of fiction and could thus be seen largely as interpretive and not scientific endeavors. This led to a wide-ranging paralysis in the field, often called the "crisis of representation."

Youth—a highly contested category, often used to refer to minors (those under the age of 18). The notion of "youth" is historically constructed, often linked to the emergence during the early to mid-twentieth century of popular culture forms such as rock and roll. "Youth" is a term that often evokes timeless innocence but is also the locus of deep-rooted social fears and anxieties. It is a category that can have profoundly different meaning across culture and class.

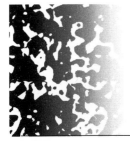

Traditions of Studying Urban Youth Culture

From the Chicago School of Sociology to Cultural Studies and Beyond

In this chapter, we explore (some) of the dominant traditions in studying urban youth culture, some of which were introduced in Chapter 1. As we will see, each of these traditions took up certain questions—for example, the early Chicago School's interest in questions of assimilation—and not others. At the same time, however, key assumptions often undergird these discussions—for example, that assimilation into "mainstream American culture" was possible or desirable and worked the same way for ethnic and racial groups. In addition, this work often perpetuated stereotypes about ethnic and racial groups that exist to this day. We will see, for example, that many studies of urban youth culture in the 1960s portrayed young black men as violent, lazy, and largely in search of sexual conquests. Tracing these traditions, as well as others, will allow us to understand what it means to study urban youth culture today. Looking at how these histories developed and unfolded will allow us to see how they could have been otherwise—opening a space for new and transformative work.

The Chicago School of Sociology and the Question of Assimilation

Like many cities, Chicago at the beginning of the twentieth century was marked by unprecedented expansion (Bulmer, 1984; Faris, 1967). Between World War I and the Great Depression of 1929, Chicago's total industrial production rose to 15 percent of the nation's total, helping to create 328,000 new jobs (Drake and Cayton, 1945, p. 228). The urban infrastructure grew quite rapidly during this period—the skyscraper, the subway, the department store, the daily newspaper all rapidly peppered the emerging cityscape in new and exciting ways (Park, 1925, p. 47). Above all else, the city seemed a site of almost limitless potential and possibility. As Frederic Thrasher wrote, "[W]e are still, for the most part, in an epoch of feverish mobility and expansion consequent upon the peopling of a new continent and the exploitation of virgin natural resources" (1927, p. 487). Indeed, the United States itself seemed at the very beginning of an unprecedented economic and cultural revolution—a new frontier.

This rapid expansion and growth was replete with both possibility and danger, a point underscored by Robert Park time and again. City life meant the breakdown of the traditional social roles and responsibilities that often marked rural life. Urban life meant new divisions of labor as well as new modes of association and new kinds of human connections around a wide range of tastes, dispositions, and lifestyles. Here, "divergent types" could reinvent themselves with like-minded others—"Association with others of their own ilk provides not merely a stimulus, but a moral support for the traits they have in common which they would not find in a less select society" (Park, 1925, p. 45). In fact, one could "map" the city's various regions as "moral areas" where particular communities of this type gelled together. People who inhabited these regions were "dominated, as people are not normally dominated, by a taste or by a passion or by some interest" (p. 45). For Park and his students, Chicago was a laboratory where "human nature and social processes" could be studied in their most crystallized forms (p. 46).

The breakdown of traditional social orders, however, also meant the loss of traditional social mores. This meant the rise of vice and of crime, a problem particularly acute for second-generation immigrants. According to Park, first-generation immigrants to the United States—Poles, Jews, Greeks, Chinese, and Italians among them—brought with them many of their Old World customs and mores. Assimilation into what were perceived as dominant American ways of life often came slowly. New immigrants tended to live together in isolated areas, largely reproducing the seemingly stable customs of their home country. Their children, however, had no such stable roots. As a result, they were often caught between two worlds, without the mooring of the Old World, trying to grope for some order in the new one.

Under the direction of Robert Park, early sociologists at the University of Chicago would undertake what is to this day the most systematic and comprehensive study of a single urban center (Hannerz, 1980). I would like to focus now on Frederick Thrasher's *The Gang: A Study of 1,313 Gangs in Chicago* (1927). In many ways, it is the first comprehensive study of "urban youth" and remains a valuable, if problematic, contribution. A panoramic, multilayered, richly detailed account of youth gangs, it remains a touchstone volume of the movement and of the moment. It is a classic of the **Chicago School of Sociology** in general and gang research in particular. As noted, Thrasher worked closely with Robert Park (who wrote the original preface) and was in constant dialogue with other texts of the time, including Anderson's *The Hobo*, Park's *The City*, and Zorbaugh's *The Near North Side*. Thrasher

Chicago School of Sociology

under the direction of Robert Park, early sociologists at the University of Chicago (beginning in the 1920s) would undertake what is, to this day, the most systematic and comprehensive study of a single urban center.

extended this interest in Chicago as an urban experiment and laboratory into new areas. His book wrestled with many key issues in this regard, including the social and spatial organization of urban centers, how immigrants dealt with assimilating into new urban terrain, and the role of gangs as social organizations. Ulf Hannerz (1980) highlighted *The Gang* as one of five key studies of the period in his book *Exploring the City.*

The Gang: A Study of 1,313 Gangs in Chicago

Youth gangs
originally, informal groups and organizations young people formed together. Over time, the term has become a more explicitly criminalized one, used to talk about more formal groups with more rigid boundaries, organized for illicit or criminal purposes.

According to Thrasher, **youth gangs** were a product of "in-between" urban spaces. They were about regulating the so-called disorder introduced to Chicago by nonnative whites and American blacks. In an article published in 1926, "The Gang As a Symptom of Community Disorganization," Thrasher echoes these concerns: "Three-fourths of the population is composed of foreign-born peoples and their immediate progeny. These diverse cultural elements have added greatly to the general confusion. Chicago is a mosaic of foreign colonies with conflicting social heritages." He continues, "There has not yet been a time for adjustment among these diverse elements and for the development of a consistent and self-controlled social order. The gang is one symptom of this 'cultural lag'" (p. 4).

The young children of immigrants, again, did not have access to the Old World customs and mores that influenced their parents—they were thrown headlong into the seemingly seediest aspects of American culture, "the more racy and the more vicious aspects," as Thrasher would write in 1927 (p. 490). There was, to Thrasher, a "blind groping for order, without much understanding of the nature of the problems involved or of their difficulties" (p. 488). This search for "order" led to the organization of what would amount to these alternative minisocieties in what he would famously term "interstitial" areas of Chicago. These areas, collectively, comprised what he would name Chicago's "gangland."

Thrasher would call the concept of interstitial sites the most important of the book. These are "spaces that intervene between one thing and another" (p. 22). He continues,

> In nature foreign matter tends to collect and cake in every crack, crevice, and cranny—interstices. There are also fissures and breaks in the structure of social organization. The gang may be regarded as an interstitial element in the framework of society and gangland as an interstitial region in the layout of the city. (p. 22)

For Thrasher, these gangs did not grow up in the "better" parts of the city but were part and parcel of the kinds of social, cultural, and material dislocations that marked urbanization and immigration. According to Thrasher, "Purely residential and well-organized suburbs of the better type such as Oak Park and Evanston, are practically gangless, for the activities of the children are well provided for in family, school, church, and other established institutions" (p. 20).

A peculiar kind of frontier imagery informs this discussion. Early on, the chapter "Gangland" takes the reader on a picturesque, melodramatic tour of Chicago—"The North Side Jungles," "The West Side Wilderness," "The South Side Badlands," and beyond. Each area was marked by unique ethnic and racial enclaves, all of which were crosscut by gang alliances and allegiances. Thrasher compares gangland to a broad "empire" marked by violence and fueled by competing interests.

> The feudal warfare of youthful gangs is carried on more or less continuously. Their disorder and violence, escaping the ordinary controls of the police and other social agencies of the community, are so pronounced as to give the impression that they are almost beyond the pale of civil society. In some respects these regions of conflict are like a frontier; in others, like a "no man's land," lawless, godless, wild. (p. 6)

Again, the imagery to describe these areas is striking in its melodramatic, almost cinematic dimensions.

Here, as throughout *The Gang,* we see strong normative underpinnings, problematic demarcations between the organized and unorganized, the normal and the abnormal, the well adjusted and maladjusted, white and other. Suburban areas such as Oak Park and Evanston were the "absent present" that served to underscore the pathologies of immigrant urban areas and families. In these areas, children ran free, outside the purview and control of adults as well as institutions that could attract them in any meaningful way. Here, Thrasher highlights the "failure of the immigrant to control his children," as well as "the lack of tradition in the American community" (p. 489).

He highlights, as well, the ways that organizations such as the church and school have failed to speak in meaningful ways to these youths. These organizations and others, Thrasher argues, all compete for the imagination of young boys— with gangs often emerging as the most attractive such group. In "The Gang As a Symptom of Community Disorganization," Thrasher argues that gangs emerge from fundamental deficiencies in family life, religion, education, and recreation (p. 7). Each has failed to provide for the young boy what gangs do—a powerful sense of self-directed freedom. Importantly, Thrasher does not locate a psychological "deficiency" in the gang boy but talks about gangs as the product of in-between areas where formal institutions have failed to take hold and flourish in ways that make sense to these youths. For Thrasher, the gang "flower[s] where other institutions are lacking or fail to function efficiently. It is a typical symptom of the disorderly life of the frontier" (p. 20).

The reform impulse here is complex. Clearly, there is a missionary zeal to much of this work, a zeal underpinned by a set of normative assumptions about the "deficiency" of immigrant groups and the unquestioned need for assimilation to American customs and mores. Of course, these notions have been roundly criticized since then. Both the desirability of assimilation to mainstream American norms and values and the idea that one can even speak of "American" norms and values in monolithic ways have been called inextricably into question. At points, Thrasher gestures toward the idea that certain seemingly pathological behaviors—for example, excessive drinking—can be located across the class spectrum. However, overall, Thrasher seems to be a man of his time, embroiled in a set of assumptions about ethnic "others" and the need for reform and uplift.

Although limited by his moment, Thrasher, it is worth pointing out, does not locate the various problems of gang life in young people themselves. In fact, Thrasher explicitly argues against the idea that there is some "gang impulse" that controls boys, that it is the product of some biological impulse. According to Thrasher, this traditional explanation of gang behavior lacked an understanding of the "plasticity" of boys as well as the pressures of social circumstance. He writes, "[Man's] nature is plastic and he excels in his capacity to adapt himself to a multiplicity of circumstances for which instinct could not fit him." (p. 43). Arguing against dominant logic of the time, Thrasher continues, "[The gang boy] is primarily a creature of habit, but the patterns of his habits may be infinitely varied in varied circumstances" (p. 43).

This concern for the social, for people's "varied circumstances," is important. Thrasher's unit of analysis for understanding young people's lives is what he calls "the situation complex," a notion deserving more acute attention than it has perhaps received. Thrasher uses the term in a few different ways throughout *The Gang*. Early in the volume, Thrasher notes that the various "conditioning factors within which the gang lives, moves, and has its being, may be regarded as the 'situation complex' within which the human nature elements interact to produce gang phenomena" (p. 144). Here, Thrasher stresses the kinds of spatial factors that both enable and constrain the kinds of activities boys can engage in. The layout of buildings, streets, alleys, bodies of water, and the like all interact to allow for certain kinds of activities and not others.

Later in the book, Thrasher moves beyond the geographical to talk about "the situation complex" in broader and more expansive ways. It is here that we see Thrasher at his most powerful and most problematic:

> Such underlying conditions as inadequate family life; poverty; deteriorating neighborhoods; and ineffective religion, education, and recreation must be considered together as a situation complex that forms the matrix of gang development. It seems impossible to control one factor without dealing with the others, so closely are they interwoven, and in most cases they are inseparable from the general problem of immigrant adjustment. (p. 491)

Pathologizing discourses

the range of ways people or places are made to "stand in for" or symbolize a whole host of social ills or problems.

Of course, we see here an extension of the **pathologizing discourses** Thrasher deploys throughout the volume (e.g., "inadequate family life"). Yet, we also see a broader effort to situate these young people's lives within a web of influences that cannot be understood except in relation to each other. The point is important. Although this book focuses on gangs, we find a constant effort to see these young boys' lives in radical context. One can understand the effect of any aspect of boys' lives only in relation to others. Indeed, while this book is, of course, "about" gangs, it is wider in scope than is much work in the delimited field of criminology (a point made by Venkatesh, 2003). It does not prefigure the role and importance of gangs in young people's lives but situates these organizations in a broader institutional matrix. As noted, Thrasher argued that we cannot understand gangs unless we understand competing institutions, including religion, family, school, and other kinds of recreation. This book, again, is a touchstone in the study of urban youths—the first such study and one well worth revisiting in detail for many different reasons.

Street Corner Society: The Social Structure of an Italian Slum

The work of the Chicago School of Sociology was largely concerned, then, with the question of assimilation into the dominant norms and mores of the American mainstream. This presupposed, of course, that there was such a thing as an "American mainstream" and that people naturally wanted or needed to be acclimated to it. This work, as noted, largely focused on recent ethnic immigrants to the United States—the Polish, Italians, and Eastern European Jews among them. Perhaps the best known study to emerge from the Chicago School of Sociology was taken up with just such concerns—William Foote Whyte's *Street Corner Society: The Social Structure of an Italian Slum* (1943), the best-selling sociological text of all time. In the opening pages of his book, Whyte writes, "In the heart of 'Eastern City' there is a slum district known by Cornerville, which is inhabited almost exclusively by Italian immigrants and their children. To the rest of the city it is a mysterious, dangerous, and depressing area" (p. xv). Indeed, Whyte continues, many Americans "have long felt that Cornerville was at odds with the rest of the community. They think of it as the home of racketeers and corrupt politicians, of poverty and crime, of subversive beliefs and activities" (p. xv). These stereotypes are reinforced by statistical data that often present the area as an undifferentiated mass of problems. The problem here is one common to all ethnographic researchers: "there are no human beings in it" (p. xv).

Whyte set out to rectify this problem in his long-term study of "Cornerville" in "Eastern City" (a pseudonym for Boston's North End). He set out to explain the internal organization of this community, the ways immigrants from distinct communities in Italy—*paesani*—set out to recreate the traditions and mores that served them "back home." These ties, however, were strong enough to sustain the first generation of immigrants. Like Thrasher, however, Whyte highlighted the disconnect between older and younger generations. He writes, "The younger generation has built up its own society relatively independent of the influence of its elders. Within the ranks of the younger men there are two main divisions: corner boys and college boys" (p. xviii). The former are from the "bottom level of society," are largely unemployed, and spend their time in "barbershops, lunchrooms, poolrooms, or clubhouses" (p. xviii). The latter are a much smaller group who have "risen above the corner-boy level through higher education." They are, in sum, "moving socially upward" (p. xviii).

Like many early anthropologists, Whyte relied on "native informants" who seemingly typified or spoke for broader groups. In particular, Whyte focused on two young men, Doc and Chick, who stood in for the corner boys and the college boys, respectively. Whyte looks at the internal organization of these two key groups, the roles they make available to members, and the ways they do and do not allow for social mobility. In this respect, Whyte's social model can best be termed "**functionalist**." That is, he sees society as a well-functioning "whole," as a set of institutions and structures and roles that exist largely independent of the particular agents who occupy them. Functionalists often liken society to a human body, with each part serving a role in a well-functioning whole. For Whyte, the roles that Doc and Chick occupied could have been played by any number of people—they just happened to play them for his study.

Whyte opens the book by noting that "the Nortons were Doc's gang. The group was brought together primarily by Doc, and it was built around Doc"(p. 3). Evoking Thrasher, he continues, "When Doc was growing up, there was a kids' gang on Norton street for every significant difference in age" (p. 3). The Nortons grew out of these groupings, largely around Doc. The ties between members of the group were largely informal and relied on mutual uses and obligations. He writes, "The men became accustomed to acting together. They

Functionalism

a theory that sees society as a well-functioning "whole," as a set of institutions and structures and roles that exist largely independently of the particular agents who occupy them.

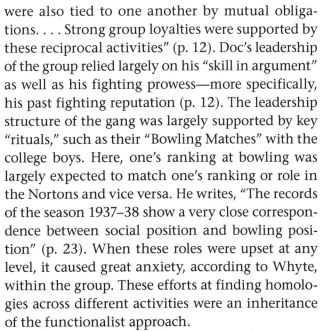

were also tied to one another by mutual obligations. . . . Strong group loyalties were supported by these reciprocal activities" (p. 12). Doc's leadership of the group relied largely on his "skill in argument" as well as his fighting prowess—more specifically, his past fighting reputation (p. 12). The leadership structure of the gang was largely supported by key "rituals," such as their "Bowling Matches" with the college boys. Here, one's ranking at bowling was largely expected to match one's ranking or role in the Nortons and vice versa. He writes, "The records of the season 1937–38 show a very close correspondence between social position and bowling position" (p. 23). When these roles were upset at any level, it caused great anxiety, according to Whyte, within the group. These efforts at finding homologies across different activities were an inheritance of the functionalist approach.

Like many early anthropologist and sociologists, Whyte thought that key informants such as Doc could tell the whole story of a particular group. For Whyte, Doc's story was the story of all young Italian men in Cornerville who tried to hold on to Old World customs and who had reservations about assimilating into mainstream American culture. Indeed, one of the major findings of the book was the way in which the kinds of mutual uses and obligations that Doc displayed—which allowed him to be a leader in the group—did not allow him to operate across multiple social spheres. These uses and obligations kept him largely local. At one point, Doc was persuaded to go into politics and run for public office. But this required that he separate himself from the Nortons—his source of social and emotional support. He ended up depressed and broke, cycling in and out of several jobs before returning to work in a local community center. In short, Doc could not translate his local standing to something broader—a key implication of the book and of the moment in urban sociology, as will soon be noted.

Whyte counterposes the story of Doc to the story of Chick. If Doc represented the impulse to stay local, to maintain multiple alliances and allegiances no matter the cost, Chick was decidedly more individualistic and more intent on climbing broader, mainstream social hierarchies. Chick was the informal leader of a group Whyte calls "the college boys," who formed the Italian Community Club. The club was established with the explicit goal of social advancement and betterment of Italians. Chick himself embodied this assimilationist impulse. According to Whyte, Chick "felt inferior" from a young age and worked hard to change his accent and improve his vocabulary. Education was key in this regard. As Whyte demonstrates, the very first issue the Community Club faced was "whether the club should admit men who had no college or professional education."(p. 97). Though they ultimately decided that they should, the exclusionary ethic largely marked the tenor of the group. Most of the social activities of the group revolved around so-called betterment. For example, the group put on plays, held debates, and sponsored smoking nights for "intellectuals."

The Community Club had two ideals in mind—individual advancement and the broader advancement of Cornerville. Yet Whyte shows that both could not be realized simultaneously. In the end, "[t]he college boys were primarily interested in social advancement. The corner boys were primarily interested in their local community" (p. 97). Importantly, most of the reform efforts that targeted Cornerville—for example, the settlement houses that came to pepper the area—were built on a model that gave privileges to the former. Cornerville was assumed to be disorganized and pathological. The goal was to help individuals to break away from the group through hard work. For Whyte, Cornerville is organized, just not integrated more widely. The goal for Whyte was to develop ways to ameliorate the conditions of so-called ethnic slums that had some integrity in the local context.

. . .

These two classic studies, in many respects, set the agenda for the next several decades of study of urban youth culture. These studies were marked by a social pathology framework. The city was largely assumed to be a "problem," one in which sociologists needed to intervene. Objects of study were often the most seemingly spectacular ones—here, the focus on so-called gangs (though the term would come to have different connotations over time). The city also was to be studied largely through the viewpoints of men in public places. The street corner would remain the locus of study—not more intimate spaces, not more domestic ones. The city could be studied as a self-contained space, seemingly shut off and disconnected from broader geographic and spatial contexts. Cities were, in this respect, little pathological "nations" within a larger nation. The distinction would serve to reinforce the seeming distinction between the so-called unmarked or normal mainstream and deviant city spaces. Finally, these studies were marked by a kind of "social realism" that did not necessarily call the research process itself into question. Power differentials between those studying and those being studied were not interrogated, nor were the realist narrative strategies of these ethnographers called into question.

The Racialization of City Spaces: The Chicago School of Sociology in the 1960s and Beyond

The next important generation of writers on cities held this largely unbroken line from the Chicago School. There were some key differences, however. Whereas this earlier work tended to focus on ethnic differences, work in the 1960s and later tended to focus on questions of race. The "ethnic other" of Thrasher and Whyte became the "racial other" of Elliot Liebow's *Tally's Corner: A Study of Negro Streetcorner Men* (1967), Ulf Hannerz's *Soulside: Inquiries into Ghetto Culture and Community* (1969), and, later, Elijah Anderson's *Street Wise: Race, Class,* and *Change in an Urban Community* (1990) and *Code of the Street: Decency, Violence, and the Moral Life of the Inner City* (1999). In short, we see the **racialization** of social problems. This work too focused on the experiences of young men in public settings. It also focused on the so-called ghetto (to echo James Baldwin) as "another," and largely pathological, "country." Although this work was certainly more circumspect in this regard, it too was largely concerned with how and why these communities were not integrated into a broader, mainstream American culture. Even as they discussed key fractures in black communities, these studies helped to calcify the notion that ghetto communities were dangerous, racially homogeneous places. Coming on the heels of the charged civil rights and emergent Black Power movements, this work looked to a country that had emerged as largely divided along racial lines. The assimilation models that had undergirded public debate around difference were no longer sufficient to address the imperatives of the moment.

Racializing discourses the range of ways people or places are marked primarily by their race, often in ways that "other" or distance them.

Tally's Corner: A Study of Negro Streetcorner Men and Soulside: Inquires into Ghetto Culture and Community

Elliot Liebow's *Tally's Corner: A Study of Negro Streetcorner Men* (1967) is one of the great descriptive studies of urban life and young men. This book emerged in the wake of Lyndon Johnson's War on Poverty and also the release of the Moynihan Report, which located many urban ills in the prevalence of female-headed households and the attendant lack of men in the family unit. Liebow set out to move beyond such public understandings of urban communities and to focus on the everyday realities (in particular) of men in these sites. Working in an impoverished part of Washington, DC, Liebow writes, "The present study is an attempt to meet the need for recording and interpreting lower-class life of ordinary people, in their grounds and on their terms" (p. 5). Such work questioned the "validity," Liebow notes, of much of the "data gathered by interview and questionnaire," (p. 8), which focused only on a narrow set of questions and problems that robbed urban communities of much of their rich context.

The result was a largely descriptive study of several young men and their roles and relationships—for example, "father-child, husband-wife, and friend and lover"—as they were lived out locally (p. 8). The point, for Liebow, is to see how these roles can be or cannot be mapped onto "middle-class behavior" and why or why not. Importantly, like many of the Chicago School studies, this study focuses on a public site where men congregate—here a New Deal carry-out shop. As he writes,

> In this setting, and on the broad corner sidewalk in front of it, some twenty men who live in the area regularly come together for "effortless sociability." . . . each man comes here mainly because he knows the others will be here, too. He comes to eat and drink, to enjoy easy talk, to learn what has been going on, to horse around, and to look at women and banter with them, to see "what's happening" and to pass the time. (p. 13)

Although about twenty men regularly hang out at the carry-out store, he focuses on a few—Tally, Sea Cat, Richard, and Leroy.

His descriptions of these men reinforce stereotypes about black men—stereotypes that largely exist to this day. For example, Tally is described as having married and then separated, lived in several parts of the city, and fathered eight children—three with his wife, and five more by five different women. Sea Cat dropped out of school, separated from his wife, and "moves with the easy grace of the athlete" (p. 14). Liebow underscores Sea Cat's unique ability to tell stories—from the grand to the mundane, he was apparently quite captivating. Richard, in turn, built up a reputation as a hard-working man who tried to provide a good life for his family. However, his life took a decidedly wrong turn. He had had several recent fights and eventually killed a man. Liebow's book is an effort to understand how these men understood their lives "from the ground up." Liebow is certainly to be applauded for the impulse, but, like many sociologists, he often reproduces stereotypes as he tries to contest or understand them.

For example, we see a complex discussion of work in the chapter "Men and Jobs"—perhaps the book's best known arguments. Liebow opens the chapter by describing a man in a truck, looking for day labor, passing a group of black men who are largely unresponsive. Many turn down his offers for work, and he drives away—his stereotypes about black men as lazy and irresponsible largely reinforced. Liebow looks to explore this decision not to work, to give it some context. He ends by arguing that these jobs are low paying, always around, and often compete with other demands. He writes,

> Delivering little, and promising no more, the job is "no big thing." The man appears to treat the job in a cavalier fashion, working and not working as the spirit moves him, as if all that matters is the immediate satisfaction of his present appetites, the surrender to present moods, and the indulgence of whims with no thought for the cost, the consequences, the future. (p. 40)

This contrasts, for Liebow, with the "future orientation" of the middle class—a disposition that implies a more robust set of options and choices about the future.

Liebow's effort here is to contextualize the decisions these men make about work. Enumerating the advantages and disadvantages of each job, he argues, these men make strategic decisions about their labor in different spheres. Retail work is steady but low paying. One can always steal from the job but still, in the end, one cannot support a family on this kind of work. Construction offers better pay but is seasonal and highly competitive. In addition, the sites are often remote and the men need transportation to get there. The work is difficult as well and physically taxing. The kinds of jobs these men can get and keep do not provide a living wage. In the end, the men end up jaded about the world of work. They are weary and internalize many of the stereotypes mainstream America holds about them—finally, each is "terrified by his experiences, his belief in his own self-worth destroyed and his fears a confirmed reality" (p. 45).

Liebow's following chapters move across similarly fraught and problematic terrain. He discusses the ways in which a stable marriage is often forgone for a series of unstable and mutually exploitative relationships. He writes that "men and women talk of themselves and others as cynical, self-serving marauders, ceaselessly exploiting one another as use objects or objects of income" (p. 89). In the face of this economic and domestic uncertainty, these men throw themselves into their friendships, friendships that are often "romanticized," according to Liebow.

> Unlike other areas in our society, where a large portion of the individual's energies, concerns, and time are invested in self-improvement, career and job development, family and community activities, religious and cultural pursuits, or even in broad, impersonal social and political issues, these resources in the streetcorner world are almost entirely given over to the construction and maintenance of personal relationships. (p. 105)

Clearly, this was not the most flattering portrait of young black men. Although Liebow tried to unpack some of why the stereotypes about black men existed, trying to give them a human dimension, he often reinforced them—a point Mitchell Duneier (1992) makes about this book as well as another classic of the era, Ulf Hannerz's *Soulside: Inquiries into Ghetto Culture and Community* (1969). In this book, Hannerz argues that ghettos, like many ethnic neighborhoods, are increasingly not places people "choose" to live in. Instead, they are places in which many African Americans are increasingly segregated, cut off from the broader mainstream. Hannerz argues that particular forms of culture arise here—ones that are not "just like" white ones or ones that should be seen as "exotic." It is this line that Hannerz tries to walk as he undertakes his study of young black men in Washington, DC.

In the book's first chapter, Hannerz takes us to familiar terrain—the black family. He argues here that the black family does not fall into the traditional, mainstream "patriarchal" model. Echoing Moynihan, Hannerz calls these communities, largely "matrifocal." He writes,

> The male placed in ghetto-specific circumstances may make unsatisfactory contributions as a provider; his ability to manage family business is small; and his wife remains in charge of domestic organization, so he does not compensate by taking over any of those contributions to household functioning that are at the basis of the mainstream wife's reasonably high status in the household. (p. 76)

The result is that "matrifocality," or "*de facto* leadership by the woman (or women) in the household" (p. 76).

As Hannerz argues, there are several ways to understand this phenomenon—that they are an extension of African cultural norms and mores, that they are a product of slavery and the breakdown of the family unit, and, finally, that they are "macrosociological" in origin—that is, they are the roles made available by dominant culture that are largely easier for women to fit into than men. In counterdistinction, Hannerz argues we must look at these practices in their cultural specificity within communities themselves. Culture, for Hannerz, has a life of its own. Among black men, several practices help constitute what he calls "the ghetto man." These include "pimping" or using women, being violent and aggressive when necessary, stressing appearance, drinking a lot, and being able to participate in verbal jousts, duals, and storytelling. All help make up the mythical ghetto man, a role that has largely arisen as a response to being shut out of dominant culture.

This role is bigger than any one individual. As Hannerz explains, men spend lots of time talking on street corners, telling stories which extol and naturalize the ghetto man. He writes,

By sharing experiences, the men establish the fact that a man can hardly help womanizing, drinking, and getting into trouble. It is all a part of the sex ascribed to him, his most important identity. Whatever the followers of mainstream culture have to say about such activities, it seems he will have to be at peace with his nature. (p. 116)

This kind of masculinity is enacted through such storytelling and boasting. Indeed, Hannerz focuses here on the kinds of rhymed boasting and bragging that many now understand as an early manifestation of rapping—"verbal contests occur among young males as well as among their adult counterparts . . . This is the phenomena [sic] which has become known as 'the dozens,' but it is also known as 'sounding' and under some other local names" (p. 129). These street-corner performances helped to reify and reinforce notions of black maleness. Such notions were reinforced in much rhythm and blues or soul music of the time, which Hannerz discusses as well. In the book's last chapter, Hannerz sums up much of what he sees in ghetto communities as opposed to mainstream ones:

Among the components of this ghetto-specific complex are for instance female household dominance; a ghetto-specific male role of somewhat varying expression including, among other emphases, toughness, sexual activity, and a fair amount of liquor consumption; a relatively conflict-ridden relationship between the sexes; rather intensive participation in informal social life outside the domestic domain; flexible household composition; fear of trouble in the environment; a certain amount of suspiciousness toward other persons' motives; relative closeness to religion; particular food habits; a great interest in the music of the group; and a relatively hostile view of white America and its representatives. (p. 177)]

For Hannerz, understanding the specificity of this culture might allow a more honest and open discussion or negotiation with the mainstream—a perhaps dubious, but necessary, conclusion in many ways.

. . .

Both of these books, then, helped to create a particular picture of "urban culture," one limited in key ways. Like their predecessors, these books were centrally concerned with how these communities did not integrate into mainstream American culture. The great effort here was to contribute to an increased racial sensitivity in this regard, to debunk biological explanations for the seeming failure of African Americans to integrate into mainstream U.S. culture. The impulse was to create "cultural" explanations that helped to make sense of life on the ground—although, again, these were limited in the ways discussed here.

Streetwise: Race, Class, and Change in an Urban Community and Code of the Street: Decency, Violence, and the Moral Life of the Inner City

The next generation of Chicago School of Sociology–influenced work—the work of William Julius Wilson, Elijah Anderson, and others—took on these questions in similar though slightly different ways. The work of both these men tended to focus on larger sociological issues—in particular, the flight of traditional working-class jobs from urban centers with the rise of **deindustrialization**. Moreover, this work did not treat urban communities or inner cities as monolithic entities, but as a staging ground for different visions for black life. Clearly normative and ameliorative in its disposition, this work extended the Chicago School project in new directions, with important implications for social and political policy.

Former Lucy Flower University Professor and Director of the Center for the Study of Urban Inequality at the University of Chicago, sociologist William Julius Wilson set the stage for much of this work. In books such as *The Declining Significance of Race* (1978), *The Truly Disadvantaged: The Inner-City, the Underclass and Public Policy* (1987), and *When Work Disappears: The World of the New Urban Poor*

Deindustrialization
the economic shift in many parts of the world away from heavy industry and physical, skilled labor. Often marked by the weakening of traditional union membership and long-term employment and by the rise of work in finance, new technologies, or the service sector.

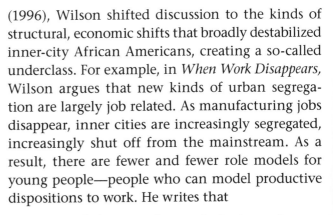

(1996), Wilson shifted discussion to the kinds of structural, economic shifts that broadly destabilized inner-city African Americans, creating a so-called underclass. For example, in *When Work Disappears,* Wilson argues that new kinds of urban segregation are largely job related. As manufacturing jobs disappear, inner cities are increasingly segregated, increasingly shut off from the mainstream. As a result, there are fewer and fewer role models for young people—people who can model productive dispositions to work. He writes that

> segregated ghettos are less conducive to employment and employment preparation than are other areas of the city. Segregation in ghettos exasperates employment problems because it leads to weak informal employment networks and contributes to the social isolation of individuals and families, thereby reducing their chances of acquiring the human capital skills, including educational training, that facilitate mobility in society. (p. 24)

We thus see the abiding concerns of the Chicago School reflected here, concerns with mobility and the production of middle-class dispositions. Unlike some earlier ethnographies, Wilson locates so-called ghetto-specific behavior in the economy.

Elijah Anderson powerfully picks up and develops these concerns in books, including *Streetwise: Race, Class, and Change in an Urban Community* (1990) and *Code of the Street: Decency, Violence, and the Moral Life of the Inner City* (1999). In these highly influential—and more explicitly ethnographic—texts, Anderson marks what he sees as a major sea change in the nature of so-called ghettos. "The interpersonal trust and moral cohesion that once prevailed are undermined," he writes, "and an atmosphere of distrust, alienation, and crime pervades the area, further disrupting social organization" (1990, p. 3). Once rich and vibrant, these communities are now marked by "unemployment, crime, drug use, family disorganization, and antisocial behavior" (p. 2). Anderson elaborates, arguing that black youths are without the role models that have helped guide previous generations, that they have been left rudderless with only the street to guide them. Paralleling Wilson, he maintains that there has been a general flight of the black middle class from urban centers and this has resulted in a loss of key older figures or "**old heads**." A new kind of role model has emerged: "young, often a product of the street gang, and at best indifferent to the law and traditional values" (p. 3).

For Anderson, these young men are largely defining street life in communities such as Philadelphia, where his research was conducted. Anderson's portraits of these young black men are none too flattering:

> For many young men the drug economy is an employment agency superimposed on the existing gangs network. Young men who "grew up" in the gang, but now are without clear opportunities, easily become involved; they fit themselves into its structure, manning its drug houses and selling drugs on street corners. (p. 244)

These young men are beyond the traditional control and purview of those who are older. Indeed, older members of the community are now afraid of these youths—afraid of the crime and violence that seem to surround them. The kinds of informal social control that often served previous generations—the notion that an elder could discipline a younger person—is now gone. The peer group reigns supreme in all matters. Even sexuality is a function of peer group validation. He writes,

> To many inner-city black male youths, the most important people in life are members of their peer groups. They set the standard for conduct, and it is important to live up to those standards, to look good in their eyes. The peer group places a high value on sex, especially what middle-class people call casual sex. But though sex may be casual in terms of commitment to the partner, it is usually taken quite seriously as a measure of the boy's worth. Thus a primary goal of the young man is to find as many willing females as possible. The more "pussy" he gets, the more esteem accrues to him. (p. 114)

Old head

an older African American man "of stable means who believed in hard work, family life, and the church. He was an aggressive agent of the wider society whose acknowledged role was to teach, support, encourage, and in effect socialize young men to meet their responsibilities regarding work, family, the law, and common decency" (Anderson, 1990, p. 3).

In many respects, we see particular notions of black masculinity ensconced in *Streetwise*. As in earlier Chicago School ethnographies of the 1960s, the portrait of black youths is often sensational, reinforcing notions introduced by Hannerz, Liebow, and others.

Yet Anderson is more explicitly concerned with the effects that these notions of masculinity have on the broader black community. He does not describe them in neutral terms, as did previous sociologists, nor does he valorize them. In addition, he describes them as extensions of broader economic shifts—in particular, the loss of jobs. But the picture he paints is disturbing, nevertheless. For Anderson, the street itself is a kind of theater where black masculinity is performed. He writes,

> The residents of the area, including black men themselves, are likely to defer to unknown black males, who move convincingly through the area as though they "run it," exuding a sense of ownership. . . . Their looks, their easy smiles, and their spontaneous laughter, singing, cursing, and talk about the intimate details of their lives, which can be followed from across the street, all convey the impression of little concern for other pedestrians. The other pedestrians, however, are very concerned about them. (p. 164)

These young black men control the streets—not the stable old heads who often are as afraid of these young men as are the middle-class whites in surrounding areas. For Anderson as for Wilson, there is an attendant loss of role models for youths, role models who can show young people how to navigate the world of gainful employment.

In his next book, *Code of the Street,* Anderson extends these concerns. More specifically, he looks at what he calls the "code of the street" and how inner-city residents live through this code. For Anderson, this code "amounts to a set of informal rules governing interpersonal public behavior, particularly violence. The rules prescribe both proper comportment and the proper way to respond if challenged. They regulate the use of violence and so supply those who are inclined to aggression to precipitate violent encounters in an approved way" (p. 33). This code operates in ways that have implications for all life in inner-city neighborhoods—for both "decent" and "street" families. The terms are stark and dichotomous, revealing fault lines within the community itself. According to Anderson, "decent families" buy into mainstream values, have strong religious beliefs, are typically patriarchal, and often police seemingly loose behavior. Decent families are future oriented. "This means working hard, saving money for material things, and raising children—any 'child you touch'—to try to make something out of themselves" (p. 38). In sharp contrast, "street families" invest more in the code of the street. According to Anderson, street families show lack of respect for others, their lives are highly disorganized, and crack often proliferates. Street families are present oriented. "So-called street parents, unlike decent ones, often show a lack of consideration for other people and have a rather superficial sense of family and community" (p. 45). The two groups have different relationships with official authority. The former show some respect and deference toward it. The latter do not. Moreover, Anderson (1999) explicitly links this "code" to the music of rappers such as Snoop Doggy Dogg and Tupac Shakur, reinforcing the notion that popular culture is inextricably intertwined with the emergence of this out-of-control, nihilistic generation of black youths (p. 36).

Many parents and children are caught in these value webs. Mothers often want their children to lead decent lives but know that "the code" is necessary for survival on the streets. Young people often want to embrace mainstream values but know they must always be on guard, must always display a sense of invulnerability. Anderson writes,

> To negotiate [the street] effectively, particularly its public places, one must to some degree be hip or down or streetwise, showing the ability to see through troublesome street situations and to prevail. To survive in this setting is thus to be some-

what adept at handling the streets, but to be streetwise is to risk one's claim to decency; for many youths, decency is often associated with being lame or square. In growing up, young people of the neighborhood must therefore walk something of a social tightrope, coming to terms with the street. (p. 144)

Again, many young people are caught in this tension—the tension between "street" and "decent" pressures and mores. As Anderson demonstrates, this tension is not always about simple access to jobs and other kinds of opportunities. Often, these behaviors are so deeply embedded in senses of self, they cannot simply be "bracketed" when such opportunities arise. Toward this end, he documents the story of someone he calls John Turner, a young African American man who is trying to turn his life around after several run-ins with the law. As opportunities arose, he often ended up subverting them—and himself. For example, Turner secured a cleaning job at a local hospital with Anderson's help. However, Turner said that the older co-workers were "on his case." He routinely got into arguments with them before finally leaving the job. While often decrying the effect of drugs on the community, Anderson reports, Turner eventually wound up getting shot in the stomach over a drug-related argument. Anderson sums up,

> An important lesson to be learned from John's story is that of the basic tension between the street and the decent, more conventional world of legitimate jobs and stable families. In John's case, when the two worlds collided, the streets prevailed, in part because John lacked the personal resources to negotiate the occupational structures available to him. At the point when the wider system became receptive to him in the form of a well-paying job, it was too late. The draw of the street was too powerful, and he was overcome by its force. (p. 286)

In the end, then, Anderson highlights the local nature of the "code" and how it limits youths' ability to transition out of their class faction.

This work, then, relied on many of the same notions that underpin The Chicago School of Sociology—including an abiding concern with how "urban culture" often impedes young people as they attempt to transition to the mainstream. However, there was a greater effort here to look at differences within communities, to look at things such as class and cultural differences within communities. Throughout these studies, however, studies that largely defined the field, the focus was on men in public settings, highlighting their public performances of invulnerability and respect. This is a point worth underscoring as we move into the next section. Although this was an ethnically and racially marked discussion, it was also a profoundly gendered one. For the better part of the twentieth century, the world of "urban youth" was one constructed almost wholly by and about men—research on young men, by men. A few key exceptions, such as Carol Stack's classic *All Our Kin* (1974), exist. Stack's study looked at the collective networks of women in a small Midwestern city—in particular, how goods and other limited resources such as child care circulated as survival strategy. Although powerful and important, the study did not wholly dislodge the ways the "problem" of ethnic and racial "others" was always already invisibly marked as a masculinized one. The lives and experiences of young women would remain marginalized for the better part of the twentieth century, always seen through the eyes of young men. This would become a central concern for scholars such as Angela McRobbie, who responded in powerful ways to similar such concerns in cultural studies.

Cultural Studies: Spectacular Subcultures

The Chicago School of Sociology largely defined the trajectory of work around "urban youth" in the United States, beginning in the 1920s and continuing throughout the latter part of the twentieth century. This was, however, not the only body of work concerned with untangling the complexities of

youth culture. Emerging from the United Kingdom in the 1970s, work in cultural studies took up such questions around youth culture, although in specific and somewhat distinct ways. This work was largely influenced by theoretical concerns around the contemporary inheritances of **Marxism**. Traditionally, Marxism treated "culture" as an extension of "class." That is, all behavior and action were determined by capitalism in the last instance, to echo the (then) enormously influential philosopher Louis Althusser. Drawing more explicitly on the work of Antonio Gramsci, cultural studies saw culture and ideology as a site of struggle, with young people both actively resisting and reproducing the class positions in which they found themselves. Scholars such as English historian E. P. Thompson, Stuart Hall, Raymond Williams, and Richard Hoggart opened up important questions about the role of culture in the lives of young people—work extended by Paul Willis, Dick Hebdige, Angela McRobbie, and others.

Resistance Through Rituals: Youth Subcultures in Post-War Britain (1976), edited by Stuart Hall and Tony Jefferson, was in many ways a watershed book of the movement and moment. Drawing together many of the figures who would be central to these debates in years following (Hall, Hebdige, McRobbie, and Willis, among them), the editors and authors focused on **youth subcultures**—groups, as Clarke et al. write, "which have reasonably tight boundaries, distinctive shapes, [and] have cohered around particular activities, focal concerns and territorial spaces" (p. 13). Scholars in cultural studies thus moved the focus on broad cultural patterns (youth culture writ large) to more specific, articulated sets of practices—for example, those of the mods, skinheads, Rastafarians, punks, and Teddy Boys. As the authors demonstrate, such subcultures are a way for youth to carve out symbolic space between the "parent" or working-class culture and the dominant culture. "For our purposes," they write, "subcultures represent a necessary, 'relatively autonomous,' but intermediary level of analysis" (p. 14). Through

---

Marxism

a body of theory that assumes the primacy of economic stratification and struggle in determining social life. In particular, so-called orthodox Marxists assume that the central human struggle is between the working classes and the ruling classes.

Youth subcultures

groups "which have reasonably tight boundaries, distinctive shapes, [and] have cohered around particular activities, focal concerns and territorial spaces" (Clarke et al., 1976, p. 13).

these symbolic subculture forms, youths try to solve (or "magically resolve") the problems of their class position. They are a way for youths to both resist the dominant order and also be incorporated into it.

This was, it is important to note, an almost wholly "classed" discussion—race and gender were not taken on so clearly. This is due in some ways to the national origins of this work. In work coming out of the United Kingdom, class was always the central node of difference and political contestation. This is in marked counterdistinction to the United States, where race has tended to be the central such node. We thus see an interesting paradox here. In moving away from more orthodox forms of Marxism, this work opened up a space to look at culture and its complex dynamics. This would, for a time, still be a discussion focused largely on class—that is, how does class reproduce itself through cultural dynamics. Yet, as this work spread out across the world—and in particular, as it landed in the United States—a space was opened to look at a broader range of cultural dynamics, including those around race and gender. This is taken up in the next section.

These were often theoretically dense and at times obtuse arguments. Indeed, Hall and Jefferson's (1976) *Resistance Through Rituals* marked a sharp split between the essays that were "theoretical" and those that were "methodological." Much of this work was concerned with developing a theory about how culture works in the lives of working-class youths—not with developing empirically rich descriptions of youth culture itself. Whereas Dick Hebdige, among others, noted the link between this work and the earlier Chicago School studies of Thrasher and Whyte, work in cultural studies was more explicitly critical and theoretical in nature. Specifically, this work was more concerned with the potentially liberating potential of youth resistance. Although Thrasher, Whyte, and others saw these forms as (bad) impediments to (good) cul-

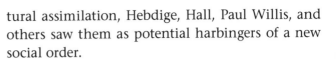

tural assimilation, Hebdige, Hall, Paul Willis, and others saw them as potential harbingers of a new social order.

Learning to Labor: How Working Class Kids Get Working Class Jobs and Subculture: The Meaning of Style

Together, *Learning to Labor: How Working Class Kids Get Working Class Jobs* (Willis, 1977) and *Subculture: The Meaning of Style* (Hebdige, 1979) ushered in a new era in critical studies of youths. In particular, these books took the everyday cultural lives of young people seriously, looking at everyday "style" as a site of resistance to dominant culture and its logics. Both located practices often deemed deviant in a broader constellation of politically resistant methods and logics. Both, however, also discussed the ways these incipient practices were ultimately recouped into the dominant culture and its logics. These works largely introduced concepts such as "resistance" and "reproduction" (for Willis) and "appropriation" and "reappropriation" (for Hebdige) to and for broader audiences. Although new political times as well as theoretical advances have opened them up to heavy critique (in ways to be discussed), these books largely set the agenda for the study of youth culture.

Learning to Labor was one of the very first books to take seriously notions of youth agency and **resistance**. Willis begins the book by asking a largely rhetorical but quite telling question: "The difficult thing to explain about how middle class kids get middle class jobs is why others let them. The difficult thing to explain about how working class kids get working class jobs is why they let themselves" (p. 1). In making this point, Willis underscores a concern central to generations of Marxist scholars—how and why are people complicit in their own class reproduction? Why do working-class people take working-class jobs? Why don't they revolt against the system? The classic answer to this question is "false consciousness"—that is, young people are dupes, tricked into not acting in their best interests.

Resistance
the everyday practices and symbols marginalized groups use to "claim space" for themselves in and against oppressive sets of circumstances.

Taking a very different approach, Willis's magisterial study looks at the cultural logics behind the decisions and affective stances of working-class youths. The decision to take working-class jobs made sense for these youths, Willis shows. In fact, leaving school and taking such jobs was experienced as liberating and empowering. Untangling these logics was the great triumph of *Learning to Labor.*

In this study, Willis followed a group of some twelve working-class youths in a depressed industrial town he calls Hammertown. Willis followed this small group throughout their school and work days, attending classes and leisure activities and, at points, accompanying them onto the shop floor. These working-class boys created a culture of resistance and opposition to authority. Indeed, this culture of opposition largely defined the group. "The most basic, obvious and explicit dimension of counter-school culture is entrenched general and personal opposition to 'authority.' This feeling is easily verbalized by 'the lads' (the self-elected title of those in the counterschool culture)" (p. 11). This oppositional culture inverts dominant values. "Diligence, deference, and respect" are all emptied of value—indeed, are actively resisted (p. 12).

Willis reads this resistant counterculture in nearly all of the everyday cultural practices of these youths—what he calls their "style." "The opposition [was] expressed mainly as style. It [was] lived out in countless small ways which [were] special to the school institution, instantly recognized by the teachers, and an almost ritualistic part of the daily fabric of life for the kids" (p. 12). These boys spent their days "dossing blagging, and wagging." Above all else, "having a laff" was key. "Opposition to the school [was] principally manifested in the struggle to win symbolic and physical space from the institution and its rules and to defeat its main perceived purpose: to make you 'work'" (p. 26). For these lads, carving out their own space in this school was a daily struggle, filled with small victories. It was not only that these lads drank alcohol, for example. They made a point of drinking it on school time, during lunch.

These boys enacted everyday resistances to all symbols of school authority—teachers as well as conformist youth. Both their teachers and such youth—the so-called "ear'oles," as they were obedient listeners—enacted and represented a kind of mental labor the lads found effeminate. "The term 'ear'ole' itself connotes the passivity and absurdity of the school conformists for 'the lads.' It seems that they are always listening, never doing: never animated with their own internal life, but formless in rigid reception" (p. 14). The ear'oles listened to teachers, deferred to school authority and all it represented. As Willis pointed out, the lads felt superior to the ear'oles, felt they were living their lives to the fullest while these conformist youth were passive and inactive. Their resistance to the ear'oles gave the lads something real and tangible in their lives. It helped reinforce the boundaries of their group.

> The essence of being "one of the lads" lies within the group. It is impossible to form a distinctive culture by yourself. You cannot generate fun, atmosphere and a social identity by yourself. Joining the counter-school culture means joining a group, and enjoying it means being with the group (p. 23).

Importantly, these lads saw school as a meaningless delay on their way to the world of real work. Importantly, the oppositional culture that these youths enacted was a culture mirrored on the shop floor to which they saw themselves heading. This was a world of physical, manual work—a world where aggressive, everyday camaraderie reigned supreme. Just as the lads tried to "get one over" on their teachers and carve out their own quotidian autonomy, shop-floor workers did the same with their bosses. "Shopfloor culture also rests on the same fundamental organizational unit as counterschool culture. The informal group locates and makes possible all its other elements. It is the zone where strategies for wrestling control of symbolic and other space from official authority are generated and disseminated" (p. 54). In valorizing work and demonizing school, the lads emulated the lives of their parents and thus their place in the class structure of the United Kingdom. Hence, the answer to Willis's opening question.

The point is an important one. Much early work on class reproduction did not pay careful attention to the everyday cultural lives of young people. Marxist theory tended to look at the structural dimensions of class reproduction. Schools and other relevant institutions were treated as so-called "black boxes." By looking closely at everyday practices and beliefs, Willis was able to show how "culture" was very much a part of how these working-class youths reproduced their own position. By actively producing the disposition of the lad, these young men felt empowered—felt as if they were getting ahead or getting one over on school authority by having a laff, often at the ear'ole's expense. This created a so-called oppositional relationship to authority, to deep investments in physical as opposed to mental labor. All this made the decision to work on the shop floor a seemingly empowering one. This, in turn, helped them to reproduce their class position. This tension between reproduction of and resistance to authority would help define a generation of work in critical youth studies.

Although only a few scholars have taken note of this (e.g., Arnot, 2004), *Learning to Labor* was also one of the very first studies to look seriously at the production of masculinity and masculine identities. The particular form of working-class masculinity these youths valorized was explicitly antimentalist; labor and gender, Willis argues, are "cross-valorized." For these youths, "mental labor . . . always carries with it the threat of a demand for obedience and conformism" (1977, p. 103). Instead, these youths chose work that allowed for "self and particularly masculine expression, diversions and 'laffs' as learnt creatively in the counterschool culture" (p. 100).

Willis documents how these young men actively produced a particular form of masculinity here— one posited against work perceived as "feminine" as well as against young women themselves. In detailing the ways in which gender identity is "performed," he opens a space to ask whether it might be otherwise. Although they did not explicitly address the implication of this insight, scholars such as Judith Butler and Judith Hamera took up this question in later years.

Willis extended this interest in the cultural lives of youths in his next book, *Common Culture* (1990). Willis documents here what he calls "**grounded aesthetics**." He writes of this nexus between the media and common culture:

Grounded aesthetics
the ways young people subvert dominant music and fashion industries by using their products in new and different ways.

> The omnipresent cultural media of the electronic age provide a wide range of symbolic resources for, and are a powerful stimulant of, the symbolic work and creativity of young people. The media help to mediate the new possibilities of common culture. Time and again in our research we were brought back to the pervasiveness of the cultural media in youth experience. The media enter into virtually all of their very creative activities. But whilst the media invite certain interpretations, young people have not only learnt the codes, but have learnt to play with interpreting the codes, to reshape forms, to interrelate the media through their own grounded aesthetics. They add to and develop new meanings from given ones. (1990, p. 30)

Willis does much to highlight the work that young people invest in popular culture and the ways in which popular culture is occluding contemporary school culture for many. Willis insistently asks us to look at how youths order their worlds, carving out space for themselves in otherwise oppressive sets of circumstances.

Dick Hebdige's *Subculture: The Meaning of Style* is another critically influential study of youths' cultural lives. Like Willis's *Learning to Labor, Subculture* was centrally concerned with the role and importance of "culture" and "style" in the lives of youths. Yet Hebdige's study was more closely focused on the **semiotics** of youth culture. That is, he was inter-

Semiotics
study of signs and symbols.

ested in how young people took the symbols and signs available in everyday life and used them in new and different ways to carve out their own, distinctive subcultural identities. If the lasting theoretical intervention of Willis was reproduction and resistance, Hebdige gave us a language of **appropriation** and reappropriation. In this study, Hebdige focused on the range of "spectacular" subcultures which emerged in London after World War II—skinheads, punks, mods, Teddy Boys, Rastafarians, and others. For Hebdige, as for others noted above, these cultural forms were a response to instability around how "class" was lived in England in a postwar context. In the absence of firm foundations, young people developed a set of subcultures to help resolve the contradictions around class. He writes, "The persistence of class as a meaningful category within youth culture was not . . . generally acknowledged until fairly recently and, as we shall see, the seemingly spontaneous eruption of spectacular youth styles has encouraged some writers to talk of youth as the new class" (p. 75).

These subcultural forms have a kind of historical specificity. For example, Hebdige offers the example of the skinheads and their emergence in England in the 1970s. Skinheads very self-consciously drew upon the traditional working-class accoutrements and attitudes of the British working class. But they did so at a moment in time when there was a "widespread renunciation of those values in the parent culture—*at a time when* such an affirmation of working-class life was considered inappropriate" (p. 79). He points, as well, to the example of the punks. At a time of widespread disaffection with the English economy and culture, the punks took the "debris" of the culture and reappropriated it. So, for example, they made fashion out of trash bags, safety pins, and so forth. This was reflected, as well, in their music, which was widely considered—even self-consciously—as primitive.

Appropriation

the ways young people take the symbols and signs available in everyday life and use them in new and different ways to carve out their own distinctive subcultural identities.

Bricolage

refers to the new ways cultural signs and symbols are "mixed and matched."

Homologies

the coherent meanings and similarities created between the different practices of distinct subcultures.

This raises the question of style as **bricolage** and as **homology**—two central concerns of Hebdige. For Hebdige, youth subcultures are key sites where different cultural signs and symbols can be mixed and matched in new and creative ways. This is bricolage. Drawing on Levi Strauss, he argues that young people can draw "implicitly coherent, though explicitly bewildering, systems of connection between things which perfectly equip their users to 'think' their own world"(p. 103). He continues, "These magical systems of connection have a common feature: they are capable of infinite extension because basic elements can be used in a variety of improvised combinations to generate new meanings within them" (p. 103). For Hebdige, young people are like artists, drawing together distinct signs and symbols and creating a coherent meaning system among them. Recall the punk use of the safety pin, the spiked hair cut, the dramatic collages—all helped form a coherent meaning system.

Style, for Hebdige, is a signifying practice—a way of creating coherent meaning out of a range of discrete signs and symbols. The links between these signs and symbols are not entirely arbitrary—there are homologies among them. These homologies help constitute the spirit of particular subcultures. He writes of punk,

> The subculture was nothing if not consistent. There was a homological relationship between the trashy cut-up clothes and spiky hair, the pogo and amphetamines, the spitting, the vomiting, the format of the fanzines, the insurrectionary poses and the "soulless," frantically driven music. The punks wore clothes which were the sartorial equivalent of swear words, and they swore as they dressed—with calculated effect, lacing obscenities into record notes and publicity releases, interviews and love songs. Clothes in chaos, they produced Noise in the calmly orchestrated Crisis of everyday life in the late 1970s. (p. 114)

Such examples point to the ways in which young people took the symbolic resources of the parent culture, appropriated them, and used them to "resist" this dominant culture. In doing so, they created a whole host of subcultures that allowed young people to find space, to live their lives, in often oppressive circumstances. "Style" here has a very important political role and function. Hebdige untangles the question of style and style in everyday life throughout this text. This was, however, a terrain of struggle. As these symbols were appropriated, the dominant culture sought to reappropriate them, to turn them into a commodity. Witness, in an obvious example, the ways in which major corporations looked to create a commodity out of punk—a process many of the seminal punk bands self-consciously, if ironically, celebrated (e.g., the Sex Pistols) or seemingly resisted (e.g., The Clash). In both cases, culture was a terrain of struggle between various interests. Like Willis's, Hebdige's work provided a framework for generations of scholars to investigate these issues.

Gendered Critiques

These frameworks, however, have certainly been challenged. From the beginning, gender—or rather, the absence of young women—was a point of contention. As Angela McRobbie (1991) notes,

> Very little seems to have been written about the role of girls in youth cultural groupings. They are absent from the classic subculture ethnographic studies, the pop histories, the personal accounts, and the journalistic surveys of the field. When girls do appear, it is either in ways which uncritically reinforce the stereotypical image of women with which we are now so familiar . . . or else they are fleetingly and marginally presented. (p. 1)

As McRobbie demonstrated, the lives of young women were marginalized in these studies, seen through the eyes of young men, and reduced to a series of demeaning stereotypes.

Indeed, McRobbie has offered trenchant critiques of both *Learning to Labor* and *Subculture*. In the case of both studies, she highlights the limitations of studying young people exclusively in public

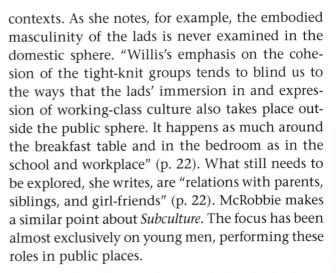

contexts. As she notes, for example, the embodied masculinity of the lads is never examined in the domestic sphere. "Willis's emphasis on the cohesion of the tight-knit groups tends to blind us to the ways that the lads' immersion in and expression of working-class culture also takes place outside the public sphere. It happens as much around the breakfast table and in the bedroom as in the school and workplace" (p. 22). What still needs to be explored, she writes, are "relations with parents, siblings, and girl-friends" (p. 22). McRobbie makes a similar point about *Subculture*. The focus has been almost exclusively on young men, performing these roles in public places.

> It has always been on the street that most subcultural activity takes place . . . it both proclaims the publicisation of the group and at the same time ensures its male dominance. For the street remains in some ways taboo for women (think of the unambiguous connotations of the term "streetwalker"). (p. 29)

In both these cases, McRobbie underscores the nature of the discussion to date about urban youth culture, beginning with the earliest Chicago School studies. More specifically, she argues that the focus on young men performing their masculinity publicly has occluded a whole other set of questions about young women and the relationships between young men and women.

In addition, both of these studies do not critique as powerfully as they might the often sexist and misogynist languages and practices of their participants. Indeed, young women could occupy only two possible (overlapping) roles for Willis's lads—"sex objects and domestic comforters" (p. 43) or, in other words, whores and madonnas. Although Willis documents the active production of masculinity here, McRobbie argues, he does not dig deeply into the lives of young women, nor does he often explicitly critique the lads' daily enacted sexism and misogyny. *Learning to Labor* is replete with hostile and demeaning talk about women, something Willis does not really take on in a sustained way. *Subculture* has similar tendencies. As McRobbie writes, "[W]omen are so obviously inscribed (marginalized, abused) within subcultures as static objects (girlfriends, whores or 'fag hags') that access to its thrills, to hard fast rock music, to drugs, alcohol and 'style' would hardly be compensation for even the most adventurous teenage girl" (p. 25). Both these texts, it seems, evidence the problems of letting young men off the hook for their often misogynist beliefs and practices.

These critiques (and others) are highlighted in Chapter 4, as "postsubculture" studies of youths have emerged as a key area of inquiry. For now, we underscore the theoretical advances of this work, the self-conscious effort to carve out a theory of youth that could account for the complex, unpredictable role of culture in social reproduction. This work set the stage (if sometimes problematically) for the scholarship on youths in an array of disciplines—communication, sociology, and education, among them—under the broad rubric of "cultural studies."

Critical Ethnography

The final body of research we will explore—the work of Lois Weis, Michelle Fine, and others—can usefully be called **critical ethnography**. These works extended and deepened a tradition that was both descriptive and deeply analytical and critical. In many respects, these works represented an important convergence of critical theory and deep ethnographic explorations. Coming out of the United States, these works extended the critical focus of the early Birmingham work but benefited from the specific political advances of the 1980s and 1990s. In particular, we see a sharper, critical focus on race and gender in these texts as important nodes of oppression and resistance. This reflects both the national and intellectual contexts of this work. On the one hand, the United States has never been as class conscious as the United Kingdom. Race and

Critical ethnography
an important convergence of critical theory and deep ethnographic explorations. This work extended the critical focus of the early Birmingham work but benefited from the specific political advances of the 1980s and 1990s, with a sharper critical focus on race and gender and the ethics and politics of fieldwork.

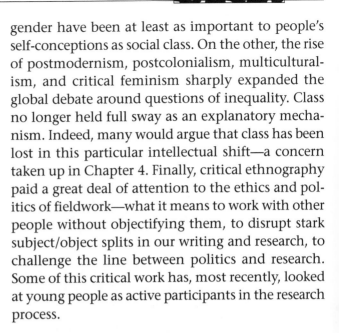

gender have been at least as important to people's self-conceptions as social class. On the other, the rise of postmodernism, postcolonialism, multicultural- ism, and critical feminism sharply expanded the global debate around questions of inequality. Class no longer held full sway as an explanatory mecha- nism. Indeed, many would argue that class has been lost in this particular intellectual shift—a concern taken up in Chapter 4. Finally, critical ethnography paid a great deal of attention to the ethics and pol- itics of fieldwork—what it means to work with other people without objectifying them, to disrupt stark subject/object splits in our writing and research, to challenge the line between politics and research. Some of this critical work has, most recently, looked at young people as active participants in the research process.

Framing Dropouts: Notes on the Politics of an Urban Public High School

Michelle Fine's *Framing Dropouts: Notes on the Politics of an Urban Public High School* (1991) is one of the best examples of an ethnography that merges descriptive explication with critical theory. Unlike many earlier studies, the unit of analysis here is more particularized—a single school. Fine moves here between rich, multilayered descriptions and broad social and cultural critiques, as she fore- grounds multiple perspectives on a single issue— the phenomenon of young people dropping out at a single urban high school she calls Comprehensive High School (CHS). Indeed, as she reports, only 20 percent of incoming students end up graduating from this school. Fine steps back and asks the ques- tion: How do we frame or understand this problem? How do we frame dropouts? Critical ethnographies such as Fine's and others often take on single such vexing issues, interrogating them from multiple angles. The movement, again, is between ethno- graphic description and broader social critique.

As Fine argues, schooling works largely to "silence" youths. Authentic and vibrant participation is not validated. In some sense, success equals silence. As she writes, "*Silencing* provides a metaphor for the structural, ideological, and practical organization of comprehensive high schools." She continues,

> Although the press for silencing is by no means complete or hermetic . . . low income schools officially contain rather than explore social and economic contradiction, condone rather than critique prevailing social and economic inequalities, and usher children and adolescents into ideologies and ways of interpreting social evidence that legitimate rather than challenge conditions of inequality. (p. 61)

This complex problem of silencing is at the heart of life at CHS. Those who are silenced typically graduate. Those who are not typically do not. Both options entail great costs—the former, mostly psychological, the latter, mostly social.

As Fine shows, charged topics such as health, sexuality, crime, racism, and economic inequality are not taken up in their multifaceted complexity. Students are often asked to think about such issues within prescribed and limiting confines, in ways that often do not make sense. Contrary or disruptive talk is not rewarded. Critical discourse is averted—talk that often contains the seeds of powerful social critique. For example, students have critiques around issues like economics, gender, and race. But these responses are often confused and despairing. Is economic marginality due to systemic or personal failure? What is the role of racism in economic mobility? Gender? Success in school means "flattening out" such discussion. She writes,

> These adolescents live in communities in which the rhetoric that stresses education as the route to social mobility is subverted by daily evidence to the contrary, and they are as suspect of the economic prospects of a diploma as they are cynical about the social distinction between "legit" and "illegit" ways to make a living. (p. 107)

Young people often develop complicated and contradictory ideas about such issues—and have no place to explore them. "They know no safe, public sphere in which to analyze, mourn, and make sense out of these contradictions" (p. 107).

In addition, many young people are often simply and unfairly "railroaded" out of school. In particular, schools are legally required to provide education for youths until they are 21 in the United States. But quite often this information is not disseminated in effective or ethical ways. Many youths and parents get the message that they are being forced to leave the school system as a whole. "At this high school the discharge process was rationalized," Fine writes, "honest, efficient, and ultimately devastating to the student body" (p. 65). When compounded by personal problems, including problems at home, many see leaving school as the most logical choice. All of these forces thus conspire to force many young people to drop out—often with the goal of getting a General Educational Development (GED) diploma, joining the military, or entering a professional or proprietary school of some kind.

Fine's rigorous ethnographic eye draws attention to how silencing works across all the various schooling mechanisms. Fine documents the ways in which teachers themselves are silenced in this process. Many of the best teachers wind up teaching to the bureaucracy—the path of least resistance in many ways. In particular, Fine outlines five discursive strategies that teachers use to deflect some of the overwhelming realities they face in the classroom. First, many teachers believe in the immutability of the current situation—quite simply, they believe that things cannot be otherwise. Second, many come to think control or discipline is the answer to the problem. Third, many come to focus on "survivors"—that is, they teach to the small number who, they believe, can succeed. Fourth, many come to believe that they simply cannot overcome the bureaucratic obstacles in their way, becoming disaffected and despairing. Fifth, some believe that they are doing the best they can and do not push further. In the end, teachers seem blocked in their efforts, locked into the same logics of silencing that affect the students. In the end, many of the best leave. With some key exceptions, the ones who stay are the ones who can teach to the system not to the students.

Like many critical ethnographies, Fine's moves between rich description and broader social critique. In particular, she argues that public schools should help nurture a rich, truly democratic public sphere. Fine calls for a kind of education that would be as "messy" as democracy itself—one grounded in social change, community biography, and people's lives and problems. Such a democratic vision does not blame all social problems on the individual. It looks toward a broader community—one "attached to collective, social action" (p. 204). As she sums up, her vision of a fully public sphere is "filled with energy, complexity, and contradiction; rich in bodies, voices, and critique; boiling with tensions; simmering in creativity; and organized through democracy" (p. 228).

Critical work such as this often pushes scholars to take on more activist-oriented roles. Indeed, the "critical" in critical ethnography pushed Fine and others to redefine their own role both in the field and at the desk. The notion that we can take on multiple such roles was developed in Fine's well-known chapter "**Working the Hyphens**: Reinventing the Self and Other in Qualitative Research" (1994) from the *Handbook of Qualitative Research*—a chapter that serves to explore and extend some of the methodological issues that undergird *Framing Dropouts*. As Fine argues in "Working the Hyphens," research subjects are typically "othered" in qualitative research. Following Clifford, Pratt, and others, she claims that subjects are made into neat fictions—often flattened-out characters in the ethnographers' imaginations. Yet, Fine maintains here that this self/other dichotomy needs to be continually worked out and worked through, thought and rethought. Researchers need to work not to "other" all those who do not fit some

Working the hyphens

term coined to describe the ways in which we are always "in between" the various hyphenated roles we have in the field—e.g., between participant and observer, or insider and outsider, or activist and researcher.

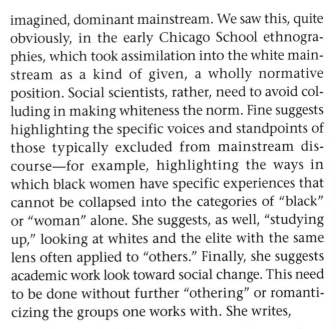

imagined, dominant mainstream. We saw this, quite obviously, in the early Chicago School ethnographies, which took assimilation into the white mainstream as a kind of given, a wholly normative position. Social scientists, rather, need to avoid colluding in making whiteness the norm. Fine suggests highlighting the specific voices and standpoints of those typically excluded from mainstream discourse—for example, highlighting the ways in which black women have specific experiences that cannot be collapsed into the categories of "black" or "woman" alone. She suggests, as well, "studying up," looking at whites and the elite with the same lens often applied to "others." Finally, she suggests academic work look toward social change. This need to be done without further "othering" or romanticizing the groups one works with. She writes,

> In the early 1990s, the whispers of a collective of activist researchers can be heard struggling with these tensions. Seeking to work with, but not romanticize, subjugated voices, searching for moments of social justice, they are inventing strategies of qualitative analysis and writing against Othering. As this corpus of work ages, it too will become a contested site. Residues of domination linger heavily within these qualitative texts. But today these works constitute the next set of critical conversations among qualitative social researchers, eroding fixed categories and provoking possibilities for qualitative research that is designated *against* Othering, *for* social justice, and pivoting identities of Self and Other *at* the hyphen. (1994, p. 81)

Indeed, the scene was set for the next decade of work—in particular, participatory action research, which Fine and others developed in new and important ways. This is discussed in Chapter 4.

The Unknown City: The Lives of Poor and Working-Class Young Adults

The Unknown City: The Lives of Poor and Working-Class Young Adults by Michelle Fine and Lois Weis is another key example of critical ethnographic work on urban youths and young adults. In this remarkable text, Fine and Weis look at both the commonalties and the distinctions that operate across the lives of working-class black, white, and Puerto Rican men and women in Jersey City, New Jersey, and Buffalo, New York. The authors argue that there has been a general loss of ground for poor and working-class young adults. From the 1960s to the 1990s, the loss of industrial jobs combined with a conservative backlash against public sphere policies conspired to marginalize young people around the country. Yet, Fine and Weis point out, these logics "land" in different ways in different parts of the country as well as for different groups. Fine and Weis look across these sites, highlighting the different ways in which different populations—for example, black, white, and Puerto Rican men and women—see the world and its issues through different eyes. This is a common feature of critical ethnographies.

Each of the chapters highlights a particular group or issue, uncovering relevant sets of dynamics. For example, the chapter on white working-class men in Buffalo looked at how they understood the massive economic shifts associated with neoliberalism. As the authors found, these men tended to perceive their relative loss of privilege in highly personalized ways—often blaming "ethnic others" for taking their jobs. As the authors note, long gone are the industrial jobs that allowed these men to earn a living wage through highly "masculine" types of labor. Instead of looking at the structural issues, these men "spoke through a discourse on work in which they drew bright-line distinctions between themselves and a largely black 'other,' constructed as lazy, unwilling to do what is necessary to get and keep a job, and content to live off of government entitlement programs" (p. 41). These men say that their neighborhoods are changing and declining, that women are encroaching on their rightful spaces, that they need to protect and fortify the family at all costs. Theirs is a discourse of loss—one they respond to by fortifying, or attempting to fortify, their privilege. White working-class men tend not to make systemic critiques. In contrast to black men, for example, they place great faith in the police to help solve crime. Black men, the authors show, tend to have more systemic critiques of police corruption and often consider the police as dangerous as criminals.

We see some important distinctions between these men and young Puerto Rican men. As these authors show, Puerto Rican men have an ongoing, complex relationship to the island of Puerto Rico. They want to preserve this unique identity while also engaging with the U.S. mainstream. This means affirming a kind of "cultural citizenship" that often translates into an assertion of patriarchal privilege. These men spoke openly about the violence in their lives and in their own childhood—often inflicted by their fathers. Yet they continued to assert patriarchal privilege. These men worked to reaffirm strong notions of masculinity, "continuing to weave fantasies of male-run households in which women stay home to do household-related chores and raise children" (p. 100). The jobs that allowed this privilege, however, are no longer available. The result is a complex constellation of national identity, patriarchy, and economic marginality—"The passion with which Puerto Rican men resolve to maintain cultural difference in the face of U.S. society is the same passion with which they resolve to be men. . . . However . . . because Puerto Rican men cannot provide for their families, they cannot keep their part of the 'gender bargain'" (p. 106).

Young Latina women are in a somewhat different position. We see these women living in the middle of a complex set of cultural pressures and discourses. These women live with a similarly strong sense of cultural citizenship, one often grounded in notions of patriarchy. Yet "we witness Latinas protesting quietly but maneuvering quickly to get themselves and their children out of the way of danger" (p. 206). The authors continue, "[T]hese women believe deeply in family, religion, and culture, even as they raise significant and profound questions about violence at the hands of men, churches filled with more hypocrisy than spirit, and a culture built on the backs of their mothers and the subordination of women" (pp. 207–208). This sense of quiet protest is marked by a deep faith in community and a profound sense of resilience—one that allows them to navigate the borders of their culture while trying to provide a better life for their children.

The Unknown City is marked by similar chapters around a range of issues (such as domestic violence and schooling) and identity positions (including those of white women and black men). Fine and Weis do not offer any clear policy response here. They do highlight, however, how these young people often work to carve out spaces for themselves in the face of this assault on the public sphere. These include the growing number of counterpublics that black and white women often carve for themselves amid economic devastation, loss of stable public safety nets, and violence. These counterpublics form in parent meeting spaces, churches, and other places—

> Engaged, daily, in the sweat and labor of living in poverty, these young women and men are finding spaces in which they can make life meaningful, pray, and maintain a spiritual soul, try to sustain a proud sense of self despite state policies that strip them of dignity, tutor their children because some schools don't, or "drag it up" one more time to attend an evening parents' meeting because "I'm afraid I'm losing my son to these streets." (p. 253)

These notions of "safe spaces" are picked up and developed by Weis and Fine in their collection *Construction Sites,* discussed in the next chapter.

Finally, Fine and Weis (1998) extend the methodological concerns raised earlier by Fine alone to more explicitly address the complexities of political activism and policymaking. They argue in *The Unknown City* that we must try to "meld *writing about* and *working with*" politically invested actors in more compelling and constitutive ways (p. 277). Ultimately, they call us to "think through the power, obligations, and responsibilities of social research" on multiple levels, accounting for multiple social contexts and concerns (Fine, Weis, Weseen, and Wong, 2000, p. 108). In the end, this kind of self-reflexivity means increasing kinds of responsibility for such questions in a social context difficult to prefigure a priori. They sum up, "Our obligation is to come clean 'at the hyphen,' meaning that we interrogate in our writings who *we* are as we coproduce the narratives we presume to 'collect.' . . . As part of this discussion, we want, here, to try to explain how we, *as researchers,* work *with* communities to capture and build upon community and social movements" (Fine and Weis, 1998, pp. 277–278). This means expanding the range of roles we play as researchers, fieldworkers, and authors, to include political activism and policymaking, roles that do not always map easily onto each other. This has been an abiding concern of critical ethnography.

Friendship, Cliques, and Gangs: Young Black Men Coming of Age in Urban America

The last book to be highlighted is my *Friendship, Cliques, and Gangs: Young Black Men Coming of Age in Urban America* (2003). Drawing on the work of Weis, Fine, and others, this book attempted to carve out an ethnography that addressed critical imperatives around inequality on both micro and more macro levels. Unlike studies that attempt more global approaches to "culture," this was a highly situated study focusing on a small number of youths. I tried here both to disrupt stereotypes about young black men and to remain faithful to the often disturbing dimensions of their lives. It also was a text that documented the fieldwork process itself, including how these relationships unfolded over time.

Friendship, Cliques, and Gangs is a deeply contextual look at the lives of two young people living in the urban Midwest over a six-year period, conducted at a community center that both attended. These two young men, Rufus and Tony, were extended family hailing from the same Southern hometown of Humbrick, Mississippi. As I demonstrate, these two youths occupied different places in the popular imagination about black youths—Rufus was "good" and Tony was "bad." Both attended a Midwest community center that was the locus for this work. Although they were similar in many ways, the two young men followed very different life courses. Rufus stayed clear of trouble, forming close relationships with the club and its staff members. Although he had not done particularly well in school, he participated in many extracurricular activities such as football and has done well in them. A very well-liked teen, Rufus received a number of awards at the club, including "Youth of the Year," as well as at school. Tony, however, had a considerably more conflict-ridden life. As he stressed to me a number of times, he had numerous problems at school with his teachers and with the law throughout his life. He spent nearly all his teen years on probation and was involved with gangs from age thirteen on.

The teens, however, were close friends—they called each other "cousins," even though they are not related by blood. Tony had a large family in this Midwest city, including numerous aunts and, most especially, cousins. Rufus, significantly, referred to all of Tony's cousins as his own. They are all roughly the same age and have been Rufus's primary group of friends for his entire life. This group, numbering roughly six, share a long history, even living together in the same house for a time growing up. This house, torn down in a citywide renovation project, was at the center of their early lives, serving as a kind of home base for the group. When Rufus's mother moved to this town from the South, she stayed in this house with Rufus until she got settled in her own home with the help of one of Tony's aunts—Rufus's godmother—who got her a job. This house was a first stop on the trip from Mississippi for many.

These claimed familial ties were crucial for both teens. I demonstrated that Tony looked up to Rufus as a person who could "kick it" or hang out with

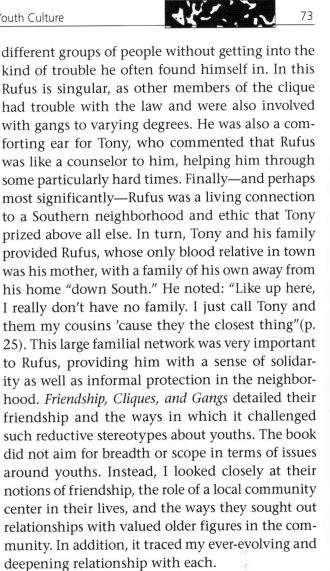

different groups of people without getting into the kind of trouble he often found himself in. In this Rufus is singular, as other members of the clique had trouble with the law and were also involved with gangs to varying degrees. He was also a comforting ear for Tony, who commented that Rufus was like a counselor to him, helping him through some particularly hard times. Finally—and perhaps most significantly—Rufus was a living connection to a Southern neighborhood and ethic that Tony prized above all else. In turn, Tony and his family provided Rufus, whose only blood relative in town was his mother, with a family of his own away from his home "down South." He noted: "Like up here, I really don't have no family. I just call Tony and them my cousins 'cause they the closest thing"(p. 25). This large familial network was very important to Rufus, providing him with a sense of solidarity as well as informal protection in the neighborhood. *Friendship, Cliques, and Gangs* detailed their friendship and the ways in which it challenged such reductive stereotypes about youths. The book did not aim for breadth or scope in terms of issues around youths. Instead, I looked closely at their notions of friendship, the role of a local community center in their lives, and the ways they sought out relationships with valued older figures in the community. In addition, it traced my ever-evolving and deepening relationship with each.

Tony and Rufus's story grew unexpectedly out of my first book *Performing Identity/Performing Culture: Hip-Hop As Text, Pedagogy, and Lived Practice* (2001), a long-term ethnography of young people and their uses of hip-hop at a local community center. This book consisted of historical and theoretical commentary as well as three extended ethnographic case studies: the ways Rufus and Tony constructed notions of place through talk about Southern rap; the ways a group of youths constructed notions of history through watching the film *Panther*, a film they connected to hip-hop culture more broadly; and finally, the ways young people constructed notions of "self" through talk about the life, death, and "afterlife" of icon Tupac Shakur. I argued in this book that reception practices—how young people picked up and responded to these hip-hop texts— were unpredictable and became more so when moving from local social networks to individual biographies.

As I demonstrated in *Friendship, Cliques, and Gangs,* my relationship with Rufus and Tony deepened and grew during this period of research. In many respects, my focus on popular culture was derailed by the immediacies of their lives and the ways in which I was called on to be a part of their lives. For Tony, providing this support meant trips to McDonald's or rides to the store or work or copies of rap CDs. After he was assaulted and nearly killed for intervening in a conflict involving his cousin, it meant visits to the hospital with various goods or simple companionship when he feared further retaliation from his rivals. For Rufus, who lived with only his mom, providing this support meant hauling large bags of clothes to the Laundromat, cashing Social Security checks, and going grocery shopping at discount stores out of town. It also included, when Rufus's mother became increasingly ill, constant trips back and forth with Rufus to the hospital, the nursing home, and the dialysis center. All of this helped me understand the importance and immediacies of day-to-day survival for these teens. I could never predict quite what these would be. But they were always extremely particular and extremely immediate.

Meeting these needs allowed me to renegotiate my particular relationship with each of these teens and also the young people at the community center more broadly. Yet the story was not a linear one, with my moving from simple "outsider" to "insider" status. As an older white male from the university, I could never have access to certain parts of their lives. But the ways we connected around their immediate needs helped open up and deepen my relationship with each. I was always,

as a result, negotiating and renegotiating my own sense of whiteness as it was read and reread through evolving everyday realities. This was a key part of this study. In addition, I was always negotiating my class status. I grew up relatively privileged, and class became more visible to me than it ever had been. In particular, it became clear to me how the most mundane of material pressures could radically alter and derail their lives. For example, Tony's glasses were broken in a fight. While he was applying for assistance to replace them—a process that took several weeks—he was nearly blind. He could only listen to TV while he recovered from his injuries. He surely could not look for work until he had them. In addition, Rufus developed a severe toothache while his mother was in the hospital. He tried ignoring it, applying tubes of Anbesol to numb the pain. But it was unbearable and he spent many nights crying, couldn't concentrate in school, couldn't work, and eventually had to have several teeth removed. In both cases, the small problems of life—the kind that I would have handled or had handled for me growing up—could alter the course of their lives. Like other nodes of power, class is often invisible to those who benefit from its privileges. Although I might have "known" this on some level going into the study, it took on a new resonance for me as this study unfolded.

Friendship, Cliques, and Gangs was, again, a highly contextual case study, one that attempted to document the complexities of fieldwork relationships. Yet it should be noted that like all critical work, this one has its own blind spots. While I tried to disrupt stereotypes about young black men, in retrospect I largely ignored important gendered dimensions in their lives—including their relationships with young women. In many respects, I fell into the trap that Hannerz, Liebow, and others fell into—as a white outsider, I paid most attention to the most salacious aspects of their lives, including their gang involvement. Like these men, I tried disrupting stereotypes but surely reproduced some of them as well. Critical ethnographers must always be aware of their own limitations and their own blind spots during and sometimes after the research process.

In sum, critical ethnography looks to uncover how power works on multiple levels, often for the most disenfranchised members of society. This work has been particularly concerned with disrupting stereotypes about urban youths while remaining honest and open about their lives. It shares Chicago School sociology's deep attention to ethnographic detail as well as cultural studies' concern with critical, theoretical engagement. As noted, this theoretical engagement moves beyond a concern with Marxism alone to a broader kind of engagement with multiple kinds of oppressions. Moreover, unlike most of this other work, critical ethnography has paid particular attention to the complexities of fieldwork and representation.

Conclusions

In closing, the study of urban youth culture has been a long and complex one. Although this story is not linear, the study of urban youths has been marked by many, often debilitating tendencies. These include the focus on ethnic and racial "others"—most often men—in public places such as street corners. This has tended to occlude the experiences of women and others whose lives often unfold in more domestic spaces. Other debilitating tendencies include a focus on "spectacular" kinds of practices and tendencies, including violent and seemingly deviant ones. Recent work in critical ethnography has tried to address some of these concerns. As Fine and Weis discuss in the afterword to *The Unknown City*, studying the mundane can be just as important and fruitful for understanding the lives of urban youths. They sum up by noting "the dull and spicy details of negotiating life in poverty. When we listen to and read narratives we (researchers) tend, with embarrassment, to be drawn to, in fact, to *code for*, the exotic, the bizarre, the violent"(p. 274). Clearly, this is a struggle, one with which all

researchers of urban youths must contend. They note, "We recognize how careful we need to be to *not* construct life narratives spiked only with the hot spots . . . like surfing our data for sex and violence" (1998, p. 274). As I hope I demonstrated with my own work and my own example, this is a struggle all researchers must engage in; it is not a problem to be solved in simple ways.

GLOSSARY

Appropriation—associated with the work of Dick Hebdige, "appropriation" refers to the ways young people take the symbols and signs available in everyday life and use them in new and different ways to carve out their own distinctive subcultural identities.

Bricolage—refers to the new ways cultural signs and symbols are "mixed and matched." Drawing on Levi-Strauss, Hebdige argues that young people can draw "implicitly coherent, though explicitly bewildering, systems of connection between things which perfectly equip their users to 'think' their own world" (1979, p. 103).

Chicago School of Sociology—under the direction of Robert Park, early sociologists at the University of Chicago (beginning in the 1920s) would undertake what is, to this day, the most systematic and comprehensive study of a single urban center. For Park, city life meant the breakdown of the kinds of traditional social roles and responsibilities which often marked rural life. Urban life meant new divisions of labor as well as new modes of association, new kinds of human connections around a wide range of tastes, dispositions, and lifestyles. Scholars were typically concerned with the ways in which different ethnic groups formed enclaves in Chicago, often bringing their "old world" customs and mores with them, intersecting with these urban pressures and processes.

Critical ethnography—an important convergence of critical theory and deep ethnographic explorations. Coming out of the United States, this work extended the critical focus of the early Birmingham work but benefited from the specific political advances of the 1980s and 1990s. In particular, we see a sharper critical focus on race and gender in these texts as important sites of oppression and resistance. In addition, critical ethnography paid a great deal of attention to the ethics and politics of fieldwork—what it means to work with other people without objectifying them, to disrupt stark subject/object splits in our writing and research, to challenge the line between politics and research.

Deindustrialization—the economic shift in many parts of the world away from heavy industry (e.g., car manufacturing) and physical, skilled labor. It is often marked by the weakening of traditional union membership and long-term employment with a living wage and benefits and often marked by the rise of work in finance, new technologies, or (most commonly) the service sector.

Functionalism—a theory that sees society as a well-functioning "whole," as a set of institutions and structures and roles that exist largely independently of the particular agents who occupy them. Functionalists often liken society to a human body, with each part serving a role in a well-functioning whole.

Grounded aesthetics—term coined by Paul Willis to refer to the ways young people subvert dominant music and fashion industries by using their products in new and different ways. This can include, for example, taping music from the radio and buying secondhand clothes and wearing them in exciting ways.

Homologies—the coherent meanings and similarities created between the different practices of distinct subcultures. For example, the music, dance, and art of punk music all evidence a harsh, "do-it-yourself" aesthetic.

Marxism—a body of theory that assumes the primacy of economic stratification and struggle in determining social life. In particular, so-called orthodox Marxists assume that the central human struggle is between the working classes and the ruling classes. For Marxists, the latter exploit the labor of the former, as they own the means of production. For Marxists, capitalism will be overthrown and socialism will emerge when the working classes reclaim these means of production and their own labor and labor power.

Old head—a colloquial term made popular in academic literature by Elijah Anderson (1990). According to Anderson, an old head was an older African American man "of stable means who believed in hard work, family life, and the church. He was an aggressive agent of the wider society whose acknowledged role was to teach, support, encourage, and in effect socialize young men to meet their responsibilities regarding work, family, the law, and common decency." However, such models have become increasingly rare, and a new kind of role model has emerged: "young, often a product of the street gang, and at best indifferent to the law and traditional values" (p. 3).

Pathologizing discourses—the range of ways people or places are made to "stand in for" or symbolize a whole host of social ills or problems.

Racializing discourses—the range of ways people or places are marked primarily by their race, often in ways that "other" or distance them.

Resistance—term that emerged from scholars associated with cultural studies at Birmingham University during the mid-1970s. Resistance refers to the everyday practices and symbols marginalized groups use to "claim space" for themselves in and against oppressive sets of circumstances. Resistant practices are often not seen by participants as explicitly political. Their incipient political importance is often located by scholars and researchers.

Semiotics—study of signs and symbols.

Working the hyphens—term coined by Michelle Fine to describe the ways in which we are always "in between" the various hyphenated roles we have in the field—for example, between participant and observer, or insider and outsider, or activist and researcher. For Fine, these relationships must always be "worked" and "worked through."

Youth gangs—term first used by Frederic Thrasher in 1927 to talk about the informal groups and organizations young people formed together. For Thrasher, these groups were a response to the "in between" position of youths in Chicago, caught between the "old world" customs of their immigrant parents and the "new world" of the rapidly expanding city. Over time, the term became a more explicitly criminalized one, used to talk about more formal groups with more rigid boundaries, organized for illicit or criminal purposes.

Youth subcultures—term that emerged from scholars associated with cultural studies at Birmingham University in the United Kingdom during the mid-1970s. In one of its earliest formulations, Clarke et al. (1976) note that youth subcultures are groups "which have reasonably tight boundaries, distinctive shapes, [and] have cohered around particular activities, focal concerns and territorial spaces" (p. 13). Examples include punks, mods, Teddy Boys, and Rastafarians.

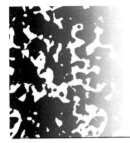

CHAPTER THREE

Rethinking the Research Imaginary

Globalization and Multisited Ethnographic Approaches

(coauthored with Lois Weis)[*]

This chapter moves from the kinds of community-based research taken up in sociology and anthropology (the kinds I tended to stress earlier) to the kinds of studies often taken up in the field of education. In particular, this chapter takes us to the contested terrain of education, urban youths, and globalization. In so doing, I put the study of "urban youth culture" inside new, dynamic research imaginaries, ones which resist the kinds of objectifications and calcifications discussed throughout this book. Along with my coauthor Lois Weis (I move between the "we" and the "I" here), I focus on the role and importance of multisited ethnography for understanding the complex, out-of-school pedagogic experiences of urban youths. I end with a series of suggestions for new directions in the study of urban youths.

In a recent volume, Cameron McCarthy and colleagues ask us to think about the ways in which

[*]   This chapter appears in slightly different form in McCarthy et al. (2008).

the "deeply nationalist, localistic and particularist beyond-a-knowing fault" project of much ethnography has been "rendered archaic" in our moment of globalizing culture and capital (2008, p. xvi). Certainly, the role of ethnography as a tool for understanding and acting upon our contemporary global moment needs rethinking in very fundamental ways. Although this has long been a concern in anthropology (see below), these concerns have taken hold in the field of education and in the study of urban youths only more recently. Educators and others interested in urban youths have tended to hold onto and locate young people's lives within a fairly circumscribed set of boundaries—home and school. In light of recent important work in geography and curriculum (see Helfenbein, 2006), however, we must consider the ways in which this project of "territorializing" young people's lives is itself a debilitating function of power. We offer this chapter as one effort to "deterritorialize" ethnography, to open up our imaginations as to what counts as education today, where it happens, and how we understand it. We offer this chapter as one example of how we as ethnographers might chart and understand our objects of analysis across a now radically reconfigured and compressed time-space continuum (Katz, 2001).

As has been fairly well established by now, the idea of culture as a neatly bounded and discrete entity has been called inextricably into question by a host of contemporary social, cultural, technological, and material imperatives. More specifically, for educators, the lives of youths now challenge simple dichotomies between home and school culture, dichotomies which have fueled much educational anthropology (see essays in Gilmore and Glatthorn, 1982). Young people now experience life at the nexus of several "competing sites of cultural production" that intersect with each other in complex ways, difficult to predict a priori (Levinson and Holland, 1996, p. 26). In this chapter, we highlight two such sites that have taken on particular salience

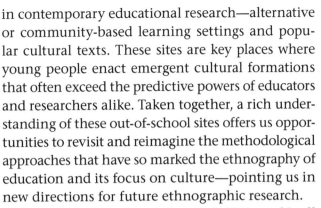

in contemporary educational research—alternative or community-based learning settings and popular cultural texts. These sites are key places where young people enact emergent cultural formations that often exceed the predictive powers of educators and researchers alike. Taken together, a rich understanding of these out-of-school sites offers us opportunities to revisit and reimagine the methodological approaches that have so marked the ethnography of education and its focus on culture—pointing us in new directions for future ethnographic research.

More broadly, my coauthor, Lois Weis, and I call attention here to the ways in which multisited ethnography allows us to draw what Cindi Katz (1999; 2001) so powerfully calls "alternative" or "counter" topographies to currently dominant ones. As globalization has inextricably separated notions of place, space, culture, and production, a wide range of social actors are being simultaneously "disorientated and reoriented" and in new and unpredictable ways (Helfenbein, 2006). Young people in Sudan and Harlem, in New York City, in Katz's key example, are experiencing life in ways that are both distinct and overlapping. Although the particular material circumstances are different, of course—one is rural, the other urban—globalization is rupturing what Katz calls "the ecology of childhood and youth" in similar ways (1999, p. 130). In both cases, the lives of young people were eroding in distinct though similar ways. Charting such links, as we discuss, also allows us to think about the question of generalizable youth experiences—a key charge for ethnography today.

Culture and Education

Studying out-of-school culture is nothing new. A long and venerable history of work in the anthropology of education contextualizes the practice of education in specific cultural sites and settings (for a helpful review, see Spindler, 2000). Formal schooling is seen as one tool of socialization, one way culture is transmitted from generation to generation. But, as Spindler and others point out, it is not the only such tool. Older and younger people engage in multiple practices of enculturation—for example, through storytelling or dinner table talk—that have critical educative implications. This work has been largely comparative. George and Louise Spindler (see, for example, the collection Spindler, 2000), for example, studied several different Native American groups in the United States, highlighting the "cultural variations that mark education in every society in relationship to every other" (pp. 30–31). Much of this work has been concerned with uncovering cultural mismatches between home and school settings. The goal, here, is to help educators in "overcoming defenses by bringing unconscious motivations, assumptions, orientations to conscious awareness" (p. 30), ultimately helping to eliminate racial bias in education through radical contextualization and cultural sensitivity.

Such work relies, of course, on specific ideas or theories about culture itself—that culture is a bounded object of study and can be understood as such, in other words, that it is discrete and can be contained. Yet notions of cultural containment belie the contemporary reality of migration, mediation, and complex cultural transactions so much a part of the quotidian for many youths in the United States and beyond. Culture—as so much work in globalization has made clear—is interconnected, in transit, the result of various, often unequally situated and disjunctive, flows and trajectories (Appadurai, 1996; Massey, 1994). As Eisenhart (2001) argues, these new tensions around culture have helped to muddle debates around ethnographic methodology. If culture can no longer be contained in discrete sites and settings, the traditional tools of qualitative inquiry need rethinking.

Multisited ethnography

"tracing and describing the connections and relationships among sites previously thought incommensurate" (Marcus, 1998, p. 14).

Multisited ethnography offers a key response (e.g., Burawoy et al., 2000; Marcus, 1986, 1998) to this muddling that Eisenhart highlights. Performing a multisited ethnography, according to George Marcus, means "tracing and describing the connec-

tions and relationships among sites previously thought incommensurate" (1998, p. 14). In any project, the multisited ethnographer must "keep in view and mind two or more ethnographically conceived sites juxtaposed" (p. 4). By way of direction, Marcus offers the following phrases: "follow the people," "follow the thing," "follow the metaphor," "follow the plot, story, or allegory," "follow the life or biography," and "follow the conflict" (pp. 90–95). All imply different starting points for tracing connections across and between different sites—individual biographies, objects, and/or stories. As he notes, "Multisited research is designed around chains, paths, threads, conjunctions, or juxtapositions of locations in which the ethnographer establishes some form of literal physical presence, with an explicit, posited logic of association or connection among sites than in fact defines the argument of the ethnography" (Marcus, 1998, p. 90). In other words, the researcher defines a question and then draws links intuitively across different tangible sites. This has resulted in ethnographic work in anthropology that has followed the same population across locations, as in, say, nurses traveling between India and the United States, or software developers from Ireland engaging in work for companies in the United States (Burawoy et al., 2000, p. 30). In education, it has meant studies such as Eisenhart and Finkel's *Women's Science: Learning and Succeeding from the Margins* (1998), which looked at the multiple sites—for example, alternative high schools, classes, and local activist groups—where women learn to become scientists.

We recall here, as well, the comparative work of Cindi Katz (1999, 2001) noted above. As Katz demonstrates, globalization is an uneven project that has distinct, though overlapping, implications for youths. In Sudan, because of land tenure relations associated with the state-sponsored and internationally financed Suki Project, "young people were unlikely to have access to productive land when they got older" (p. 133). Although gainfully employed for the moment, "children and adolescents were not learning what they were likely to need to know in their adulthoods" (p. 133). In Harlem, the structural "disinvestments in manufacturing, shipping, and warehousing along with declines in construction and infrastructural maintenance" have "dimmed the prospects for reasonably well-paying, stable employment, and most certainly of meaningful work, of many working-class young people" (p. 134). Here, too, young people were not getting the kinds of educational opportunities they would need to function in the so-called new economy. Reading these cases against each other allows us to think through and create other kinds of stories about how globalization is affecting youths writ large. It allows us another way to think about how to rechart or map relationships between disparate sites.

The gesture is important. The ability to create topographical knowledge, Katz writes, is critical to the "imperial projects glossed as globalization" (2001, p. 2). Indeed, imperialism itself was an effort to divide up and remap the contours of the world writ large, a project buttressed by the modernist discipline of anthropology (Kamberelis and Dimitriadis, 2005). At the heart of anthropology was a "monumentalist" impulse (Rosaldo, 1990), as noted, an impulse to sort, categorize, and naturalize cultural and national borders, to create clear isomorphic relationships between spaces, places, and cultures (Clifford, 1997). Much of anthropology's disciplinary work has been in maintaining these borders. As these borders are a function of power, creating counter-topographies is a way to resist and rewrite them. Connecting the experiences of youths in Sudan and Harlem thus allows us to understand both the specific ways globalization is playing out on the ground as well as how broader processes are unfolding across sites.

Such multisited projects also hold great potential to address the ever-vexing question of how ethnographers can make their empirical material generalizable. As Michelle Fine notes, many social scientists have been overly "concerned with the technical specificity of empirical generalizability"—that is, the question of formally and technically replicating studies—"and underconcerned with generalizability of theory and action" (2006, p. 98). According to Fine, the latter means talking in more open-ended ways about how our ideas and experiences evoke similar issues across different sites. Multisited ethnography gets us closer to what Fine calls "**theoretical generalizability**"—a way to "deeply investigate what about [our] findings resonates (or not) in particular settings." Even more broadly, Fine takes us from this notion of theoretical to provocative generalizability. Echoing the work of Maxine Greene, Fine maintains that looking across sites allows us to "to move [our] findings toward that which is not yet imagined, not yet in practice, not yet in sight." This means stretching out, looking past the "what is" to "what might be," (2006, p. 100) "writing research in ways that moves readers to think through implications, actions, collusion, social responsibility and social imagination" (2006, p. 102)

The "work of the imagination" is key here (Appadurai, 1996). Indeed, multisited ethnography is not simply "a set of *methods* that are very specifically prescriptive for the conduct of fieldwork" (Marcus, 1998, p. 6). It has also challenged us to rethink our **research imaginary** more broadly, implying a kind of self-reflexivity about how particular ethnographic sites are imagined, how objects are delimited. Marcus argues, in fact, that multisited ethnographies can be constructed around a single "strategically selected locale." Such ethnographies treat "the system as background," though they try not to lose sight of the fact that "it is integrally constitutive of cultural life within the bounded subject matter" (p. 172). As a key example of this kind of reconfigured multisited ethnography, Marcus offers the well-known school ethnography, *Learning to Labor*. Although the primary site for this research is a single school, Willis juxtaposes and explores

---

Theoretical generalizability

concerned with the ways our research findings and experiences are similar to or different from the findings and experiences of others over time and place.

Research imaginary

the aesthetic space in which we conceive our objects of study or analysis.

(largely through self-report data) a small group of working-class lads, as well as working-class conformist youths across sites including school, the shop floor, home, the dance hall, and local bars. All sites are put into dialogue with one another to explain how class structures are reproduced and validated through and in everyday cultural practices. Willis makes every effort to explain larger issues of class through his rich ethnographic description of young people—although, as Marcus points out, without similar immersion in multiple sites, Willis risks reproducing "canned visions of capitalism," a point we return to toward the end of this chapter (p. 45).

In sum, multisited ethnographic work—even work focused on a single strategically selected locale—has challenged us to rethink fundamentally our research imaginary in school research in ways that push the borders of the home/school nexus. Here, we interrogate two sites which resonate deeply in contemporary ethnographic research in education—community-based learning sites and popular cultural texts. We call attention to the new critical energies at work in the sites and the particular challenges they offer contemporary education researchers. Both are sites where young people's lives are being explored in ways that look beyond simple home/school entities. Both also reflect our own particular research agendas (Dimitriadis, 2001; Dimitriadis and McCarthy, 2001; Dimitriadis and Weis, 2001; Fine and Weis, 1998; Weis and Fine, 2001). We explore them both for their own potential as well as the ways in which they are illustrative of a larger set of issues, hoping to wedge open discussion and broader theoretical concerns. We begin with a look at community-based organizations and "safe spaces."

Community-Based Learning Settings and "Safe Spaces"

Shirley Brice Heath's *Ways with Words: Language, Life, and Work in Communities and Classrooms* (1983) is, of course, a germinal text in the area of home/school connections. Here, Heath looks at home language practices across three differently situated communities, noting which kinds of practices prepare students in what kinds of ways for success or failure in school. Different students possess different kinds of literacy skills, rooted in home practices, which are differentially valued or validated in school. Focused on the variable nature of literacy, this work opens up a range of questions and concerns related to language, learning practices, and specific institutions, including cross-case comparisons between and across dominant and nondominant learning settings.

Heath (2001) and her colleagues have extended this work over the past several years to focus on what they call **community-based organizations (CBOs)**, highlighting the ways in which community is the "third area beyond school and family" for school researchers (p. 15). Focusing on the organizations young people identified as most successful, and deploying what they call "guerilla ethnographers," Heath and McLaughlin spent five years looking at 60 different organizations, gathering data from 24,000 youths in predominantly low-income and marginalized community settings across the country (Heath and McLaughlin, 1993, p. 5). This research serves to establish the critical importance of these sites as well as identify key characteristics of the most successful such organizations (McLaughlin, Irby, and Langman 1994), stressing the key notion that community-based organizations are not bureaucratic institutions, as (typically) are schools, but are emergent and unpredictable. These institutions draw on the strengths of particular young people, working with particular adults, on specific tasks, with real risks and real consequences in specific settings. CBOs typically offer young people the opportunity to work through real-world

---

Community-based organizations (CBOs)

out-of-school sites such as community centers or churches where young people chose to spend their free time. CBOs typically offer young people the opportunity to work through real-world activities that demand their full participation.

activities that demand their full participation. As Heath (2001) notes,

> Community organizations that create positive learning environments exhibit these same features. Work takes place within a "temporal arc," with phases that move from planning and preparation for the task ahead; to practice and deliberation along with ample trial-and-error learning, to final intensive readiness for production or performance; and, ultimately, to a culminating presentation of the work that has gone before. (p. 12)

CBOs may include arts-based activities, such as theater, dance, and music (Ball and Heath, 1993) as well as sports-based activities, such as gymnastics, baseball, and basketball (Heath, 1991; Mahiri, 1998). If, for example, they are putting on a drama to raise money for a trip, young people have to decide (among other things) who will design the costumes, who will design the sets, who will act, write, advertise, manage the finances, and so forth. These activities unfold under the guiding hand of older, better-skilled community workers or "wizards" (McLaughlin, Irby, and Langman, 1994), individuals who see young people as resources to be used not problems to be managed (Dimitriadis and Weis, 2001).

By way of example, Heath looked at the everyday talk of a coach (Victor Cage) and his community center–based basketball team ("The Dynamos") as they worked through their season. Here, the coach modeled conditional "what if" phrases as they worked to co-create a set of flexible rules and strategies so as to accomplish specific tasks. This kind of work depends on "carrying distributed knowledge, shared skills, and discourse patterns through a project over a period of time" (Heath, 1996, p. 247). As Heath notes, the team internalized a set of rules that they were able to adapt flexibly when the coach transgressed them. Ultimately, the team created a "sense of place with a keen notion of the role of rules and ways of planning and talking about relations between rule setting and rule breaking" (p. 246).

This work has been marked by a split between school and nonschool settings. According to Heath (1996), schools often prefigure relevant curricula based on simple notions of identity, assuming, for example, that young people desire activities defined by adults as ethnically or culturally relevant. According to Heath and McLaughlin, community-based organizations thrive on the complex, already-existing social networks of young people—their ability to mobilize specific sets of personal resources to deal with concrete concerns and challenges. Lived identities in these organizations, as Heath and McLaughlin (1993) argue, are "complex, and embedded in achievement, responsibility, and . . . immediate support network[s]" (p. 32) in ways that exceed the easy delineation of (multi)cultural borders and boundaries. There is nothing predictable or stable about the ways ethnicity and identity play out in these organizations, nor do these organizations make a priori assumptions about young people and culture (p. 20). "Community organizations, particularly those in which the arts are intensely integrated, generate unexpected contexts and collaborations that often add up to some outcomes that are tough to achieve elsewhere: blurring lines of racial and ethnic division and crossing linguistic barriers" (Heath, 2001, p. 16).

For the most part, then, Heath and her colleagues have not situated their research in schools. One gets the sense—with only occasional exceptions (e.g., Heath and McLaughlin, 1994)—that schools are a vestige of another era and that for disenfranchised youths, in particular, the most interesting and important kind of education is happening outside of school. "Schools," they sum up, "are experienced as hostile and demeaning environments where neither inner-city youth nor their interests are taken seriously" (McLaughlin and Irby, 1994, p. 305). Furthermore, schools are no longer training youths for the kinds of flexible problem-solving activities which are so necessary for job readiness in the information age. Such work, again, is happening in CBOs.

Although less focused on skills, similar ideas have been developed by Michelle Fine, Lois Weis, and colleagues on **safe spaces** (Dimitriadis and Weis, 2001; Fine and Weis, 1998; Hall, 2001; Weiler, 2000; Weis and Fine, 2000). Not marked by the same split between in-school and out-of-school settings, Fine and Weis's work has focused on the imaginative resources young people use to carve out spaces for themselves in different settings, both inside and outside of school. Young people, they argue, carve these safe spaces in a variety of sites—in school and out of school—creating "counterpublics," to use Nancy Fraser's term, ironically out of the very exclusionary practices of the public sphere. "These spaces are not just a set of geographical/ spatial arrangements but, rather, theoretical, analytical, and spatial displacements—a crack, a fissure, a fleeting or sustained set of commitments. Individual dreams, collective work, and critical thoughts are smuggled in and reimagined" (Fine, Weis, Centrie, and Roberts, 2000, p. 132). Refusing the school/nonschool entity, these authors explore how young people take up public spaces (Kelley, 1997) and how they carve out private ones within the context of great poverty and the dismantling of the public safety net.

By way of example, the authors juxtapose two sites, Molly Olga, a neighborhood art center in Buffalo and an Orisha spiritual community in New York City (Fine, Weis, Centrie, and Roberts, 2000). In the first site, a diverse group of participants meet in an urban community to work under the tutelage of its director, Molly Bethel. Molly Olga's poly-vocal feel encourages people who do not normally interact with each other—from poor black youths to white upper-middle-class housewives—to discuss common concerns. It is a thriving "community of difference" constituted through aesthetic practice. In the second example, the authors highlight the

Safe spaces
imaginative and literal spaces young people turn to, to "carve out" space for themselves in often oppressive circumstances. They are spaces of healing and nurturance where "counterpublics" can be formed.

micromoves of a "self-consciously heterogeneous spiritual community" in New York City as participants invent and reinvent religious practices of the African and Cuban diaspora, making them relevant for broad groups of urban dwellers. In both cases, the authors highlight "spaces in which 'difference' signals interest, engagement, commitment, and opportunity" that look beyond the "walls of school" (p. 149).

Additional work focuses more specifically on school culture. Weis and Fine (2001), for example, juxtapose the powerful day-to-day work within two in-school sites—an abstinence-based sex education program and a detracked and racially integrated world literature class, both located in schools. In the first example, the authors demonstrate how the program participants stretch beyond the official intent of the program (abstinence only) to "traverse a variety of subjects regarding race, gender, sexuality, and men." Under the guidance of the program's leader, Doris Carbonell-Medina, this weekly meeting becomes a safe space for these young women as they discuss salient issues in honest and personally meaningful ways. In the second example, the authors show how a world literature class can be a powerful space in which to engage questions of identity and difference. "Students have learned," they write, "to engage in this space, for 45 minutes a day, with power, 'difference,' and a capacity to revision. Some with delight and some still disturbed, but they know that everyone will get the chance to speak and be heard." The authors go to great lengths to trace the discourse as it evolves over a year-long period as students discuss books such as *Of Mice and Men, Two Old Women,* and *La Llorana.*

There is, as well, a small but important body of work that has documented the critical liberatory potential of the arts for youths in that activities involving arts offer safe spaces, both inside and outside of school. For example, Michelle Fine has engaged youths in creatively documenting the legacy of the *Brown v. Board of Education* decision.

Across gender, race, and class, these young people created powerful poems and oral histories that evoked this largely contested legacy (Fine, 2004). In another key example, Jennifer McCormick's *Writing in the Asylum* (2004) discusses the important ways in which poetry and art function both in formal and informal ways in a working-class New York City high school. Drawing on the experiences of three young women, McCormick discusses the importance of self-narration and expression in the face of the profound surveillance and assessment. This work has discussed the ways the arts can give marginalized youths a voice in highly oppressive sets of circumstances.

Rather than assuming a priori parameters, work on CBOs and safe spaces raises important questions as to where education is happening today. Juxtaposing in-school and out-of-school sites, this work powerfully reframes contemporary educational questions and agendas. For Heath and McLaughlin and their colleagues, this has meant an elaborated discussion of what kinds of skills are fostered in these sites and how these skills translate across the kinds of tasks most associated with our contemporary information age. For Weis and Fine and their colleagues, this has meant looking at how a variety of young people "homestead," or claim authentic and meaningful spaces and identities within a variety of sites, both in school and out. This work intentionally decenters the home/school dichotomy in educational research, evoking the many ways in which "community" is a "third area" of study (Heath, 2001, p. 15).

Popular Culture

Popular cultures and technologies

the range of affectively charged texts, practices, and technologies young people actively turn to, to make sense out of their lives today.

Further pushing the question of contemporary out-of-school curricula, recent research has stretched well beyond the home/school dichotomy in its growing focus on **popular cultures** and technologies. In parallel fashion to research on alternative learning sites, this work has challenged our assumptions about what count as educational curricula or

texts for young people. Indeed, as a range of scholars have argued, popular culture increasingly offers a terrain upon which young people are navigating their lives and meeting their everyday needs and concerns (Dimitriadis, 2001). These cultural texts are proliferating in complex ways in and through video, film, television, and music technologies, as well as computers and the Internet—all of which have increasingly complex relationships to and with each other.

Recent work on popular culture and education has looked at how young people have used these texts in practice or performance (Buckingham, 1993, 1996, 1998; Buckingham and Sefton-Green, 1995; Tobin, 2000). David Buckingham and Julian Sefton-Green, for example, have treated media literacy as a kind of symbolic social action. Their work has explored how young people mobilize popular texts as discursive resources in particular and meaningful ways, using them to negotiate senses of self and community. In *Cultural Studies Goes to School: Reading and Teaching Popular Media* (1995), Buckingham and Sefton-Green offer several case studies of young people using the media to create personally relevant texts—from magazines to photographs to popular music—as they author their lives, so to speak. "In adopting 'critical' positions in discourse, in staking out their tastes and identities, and in intervening directly in popular cultural forms," they write, "these [youth] are actively defining themselves in relation to wider social, cultural, and ideological forces" (p. 82). This is a less defensive approach than many current media literacy approaches (see Brunner and Tally, 1999). In fact, Buckingham (1998) noted that this kind of work often invites problematic kinds of pleasures from students. Even these—perhaps especially these—must be understood if we are to engage with the lives of young people in authentic ways.

Sefton-Green (1998, 1999) extends this work, focusing on the relationship between popular media culture, the arts, and the Internet. In *Young People,*

Creativity and New Technologies (1999), Sefton-Green gathers recent theoretical and empirical work "to describe the opportunities digital technologies offer for communicating, disseminating and making culture as well as acting as a vehicle for personal and collective self-expression" (p. 1). Among other topics, contributors discuss multimedia memoirs, self-produced CD-ROMs, online school scrapbooks, and personal Web pages. These new and creative uses of information technologies are part of a broader redefinition of youth culture that has implications for all manner of educational practice—from the classroom to the dance floor and beyond (Sefton-Green, 1998).

More recently, Steven Goodman (2003) looked at the ways in which digital video allows young people to speak back to media and educational institutions that would otherwise make them passive receptors of information. In *Teaching Youth Media: A Critical Guide to Literacy, Video Production and Social Change,* Goodman documents an important critical literacy project, Educational Video Center (EVC) at East City High School, in which young people took video cameras into their own communities to document their own experiences and the experiences of those around them. The entire process—from filming to final editing to public presentation—allowed young people to work with, manipulate, and calibrate popular, symbolic resources in new and different ways. Goodman sums up, "The documentary-making process gave the East City High School students something they rarely found at school or elsewhere in their lives: a victory . . . With their video, the students could literally show off their ideas and creativity to teachers, family, friends, neighbors, and whomever else they could get to watch it" (p. 99).

More recently scholars in education have moved toward less prefigured, ethnographic approaches that look at the ways young people construct identities through popular culture and their implications for school life (Dimitriadis, 2001; Dolby, 2001; Yon,

2000). For example, my recent work (2001) has looked at how young people construct notions of self, history, and place through their uses of hip-hop texts, focusing on how these young people use these texts in concert with—and in distinction to—school texts. For example, I looked at the ways in which two teenagers constructed notions of a Southern tradition through their use of Southern rap texts; how young people constructed notions of history through viewing the film *Panther* (1995), directed by Melvin Van Peebles, a film they connected to hip-hop culture more broadly; and how young people constructed powerful senses of self through talk about the life and death of icon Tupac Shakur. All are examples of popular culture's reach and power. "We see popular culture," I wrote, "more and more, providing the narratives that young people are drawing on to deal with the issues and the concerns most pressing in their lives." "These investments," I showed, "played out in often unpredictable ways" (2001, p. 120).

Dolby and Yon have developed similar ethnographic projects in the field of education, though both have looked to settings outside the United States. Dolby (2000, 2001), in a particularly fascinating study, looks at how young people at a high school in South Africa ("Fernwood High") negotiate ideas about race in the aftermath of Apartheid. Here, music and fashion became ways to carve out ideas about being white, black, or colored at a moment when a priori racial categories are called into question. These popular symbols circulated and were ascribed different meanings at different times. Rave music, for example, "is understood specifically as 'white' music. A coloured student who listens to rave would be ostracized by her or his classmates, and seen as a threat to 'coloured' identity" (2000, p. 206). In sum, Dolby argues, "'Race' at Fernwood reinvents itself (as it does constantly) as a site of identification that takes its meaning, in large part, from affect and affective investments. Students are invested in the emotions of desire that surround consumptive practices, particularly the practices of global youth culture" (p. 203).

Yon, in turn, looked at a multiethnic high school in Toronto ("Maple Heights"), focusing on the ways in which young people negotiate their day-to-day identities. Yon offers portraits of different young people and the creation of complex identities through their investments in popular culture. He writes, "Many of the signs and symbols of the popular cultures of these youth, like dress codes and musical tastes, are racialized. This means that the signifiers of race can also change with the changing signs of culture and identity, and what it means to be a certain race is different from one context to the next" (2000, p. 71). Yon offers several examples of young people constructing notions of self through popular culture. These include a Canadian-born black, a white youth who identifies with black culture, as well as a black immigrant from the Caribbean—all of whom use popular culture to negotiate and stake out particular senses of self.

Broadly beyond the field of education, several researchers and scholars have looked at the ways popular cultural forms can serve as pan-ethnic and racial nodal points in the lives of young people. For example, Robin Sylvan's *Trance Formation: The Spiritual and Religious Dimensions of Global Rave Culture* (2005) traces the emergence and proliferation of rave culture as a site of social and personal transcendence—a site where diverse and heterogeneous young people come together to enact (often) life-changing rituals. Deeply embedded in music, dance, fashion, and other aesthetic registers, these events can be powerful examples of "unity in diversity," Sylvan writes. "Time and again, ravers spoke of how the powerful peak experience on the dance floor broke down traditional boundaries of race, class, ethnicity, nationality, religion, age, gender, sexual orientation, and so forth, bringing everyone together in an ecstatic unity that transcended these differences" (p. 180). These too are pedagogical spaces, spaces where young people enact social, cultural, and religious formation which exceed those ones narrowly delimited in school settings.

In sum, Dolby and Yon (among others) make it clear that we cannot understand young people's identities in predictable ways. More and more, as this work makes clear, we must ask ourselves what kinds of curricula—broadly defined—young people draw on to understand, explain, and live through the world around them. This is messy terrain, one that extends beyond a priori notions about identity often privileged by educators. As these authors make clear, the multiple uses to which popular culture is put challenge and belie easy notions of "cultural identification." Young people in the United States and around the world are elaborating complex kinds of social and cultural identifications through music such as hip-hop and techno in ways that challenge predictive notions about texts, practices, and identities. "The global context of popular culture," Dolby (2001) writes, is critical for "the marking of racialized borders, and for their subsequent displacement and rearrangement" (p. 9).

New Trajectories

As this research demonstrates, and as anthropologists have long noted, education takes place both within and beyond the boundaries of school. Today though, education is an increasingly emergent phenomenon, unfolding across numerous sites and settings with and between multiple texts. It is the "in-between"—the moving back and forth between sites and texts—that increasingly defines our children's lives and cultural landscapes and must, therefore, define our research agenda with urban youths.

Yet, multisited work in education has not, for the most part, explored these sites, literal or otherwise, as existing in dynamic interrelation to other sites in specific and particular ways. Although we have many studies of single sites, we do not have a sense of how these sites are enmeshed in particular ways in complex webs of relationships for their participants. We have one kind of mapping here; one where sites take on meaning in the context of other isolated sites as well as self-report data on the "backstage knowledge" of participants. Missing, it seems, are more relational kinds of studies—studies that, for example to return to Marcus, follow the people, follow the biographies, or follow the story in complex and inevitably unpredictable ways.

Indeed, while Heath and McLaughlin have suggested looking away from traditional schools and focusing only on CBOs, there seems a danger of reifying these sites as objects of study. Just as *Learning to Labor* (Willis, 1977) often reproduced canned ideas about capitalism, we are perhaps in danger here of reproducing clichés about what happens in schools if we rely only on participants' self-report data about these sites. Instead of turning away from the study of schools we suggest figuring out, in particular and situated ways, the relationship *between* multiple sites—schools, community centers, job sites, and so forth—and the skills they encourage and enable for young people. This means actually doing the research across sites in a way that we have not done before. In addition, although Weis and Fine included in-school and out-of-school sites in their work, there is a parallel danger of focusing on single-sited studies in isolation from one another, as Weis and Fine (2000, 2001) tend to do. Although these authors have taken great pains to show internal dynamism around identity within these sites, we have little sense of how participants live their lives *across and between* sites. If identity is always an emergent construction, we need to understand more clearly how these identities play out in relation to and with each other in the space of the "in between."

Like work on CBOs and safe spaces, work on popular culture and education has overwhelmingly been single sited. For example, studies by myself (2001), Dolby (2001), and Yon (2000) focus on single settings—a community center and two high schools, respectively. In each case we gain a clear picture of a particular educational site and a specific group of young people. In each of these cases, we are asked to expand our notion of education—where it happens and with what texts. Yet we get little sense of how different sites—understood on their own terms—invite the working across that we discuss here. For example, while I talk about my participants' experiences in "traditional" schools, I rely largely on self-reported data rather that entering the school site firsthand. In turn, neither Dolby nor Yon look at young people's uses of these texts in ways that extend beyond school settings. Missing, it seems, is research that follows individuals and groups—urban youths—as they traverse a wide range of texts in different settings, and, perhaps, at different times of their life.

Reengaging with the power and limitations of the work discussed throughout this chapter, we offer here a beginning set of imagined possibilities for engaging in the kind of ethnographic work discussed above. Ethnographies that recognize and take seriously into account the many sites of education can help to work against naturalized frames, categories, and theories in education—offering an important advance in our thinking about youths and schooling. Indeed, we must be responsible for the questions we ask and stretch beyond the taken-for-granted categories and assumptions. There is no neutral terrain here. How we frame problems and objects of study can reproduce unfair power relationships in our work. With multisited ethnography, we can both denaturalize our object of study and conduct powerful work in the field—a twin imperative for our continued relevance. We ask readers to imagine with us what such work might look like and invite continued discussion. The following list is meant only as a beginning for imagined possibilities.

1. We begin by calling for more studies of different groups in ostensibly the same space. In other words, it is critically important that we under-

stand how teen men and women appropriate an array of popular cultural texts and programs, for example. This project must be stretched to involve teen men and women of different races, ethnicities, sexualities, and social classes—all the time, following Heath, McCarthy, and others, questioning our a priori assumptions here. Understanding how different groups across and within race, for example, make meaning of texts or programs is an important project. We know from our own work that there is no single "African American," for example, appropriation of a text. Instead, different groups *within* any given category work texts very differently. This needs to be built within a new research imaginary.

2. As noted throughout, we would also encourage more studies of youths across spaces such as community centers and popular culture, as well as school, family, and so forth. Often we go into one such site while ignoring all others, or rely upon self-report data as to individual/group behavior in sites other than the one in which we are physically immersed. We have engaged in such single-site studies ourselves (myself in community centers and with popular culture; Weis in community centers and schools) and understand full well the difficulties of following youths through varying paths of action. Nevertheless, we suggest that we must begin to do this work. This might involve a team of researchers, perhaps one person in the school, one in the families, and so forth. Again, we understand full well the difficulties of establishing rapport and trust, even for one person, much less a team of people. But we must begin to think along these lines to explore the range of action in youths' lives and urge others to join with us as we pursue these ideas.

    These two suggestions are grounded largely in the above discussion. It is important to note, however, that multisited work has an important temporal and regional component, as well. As

George Marcus (1998) notes, it gives us important ways to understand the often disjunctive and uneven distribution of social, cultural, and material imperatives. The following three suggestions offer ways to push further the important implications of multisited ethnography, in ways we have not yet discussed.

3. As we have indicated throughout this chapter, we see great possibilities in following the people or following the individual across sites and texts. Most ethnographic studies, however, are inevitably done at a single point in time at a single site. Although we do learn a great deal from such studies, what we do not know is what happens to them after they leave these specific locations. Culturalist theoretical challenges, although important, do not enable us to probe the linkages between actual school experiences as explored by ethnographers and life chances and choices in other sites. Thus, multisited work in education could powerfully be conducted over time as well as space. We have some examples of follow-up studies, such as Jay MacLeod's *Ain't No Makin' It: Aspirations and Attainment in a Low-Income Neighborhood* (1995), Claire Wallace's *For Richer, For Poorer* (1987), and Paul Willis's *Learning to Labor: How Working Class Kids Get Working Class Jobs* (1977). These studies, however, tend to be short-term follow-ups. Willis, for example, followed his subjects only briefly into the work force. Although we certainly understand why it is that investigators do not engage in long-term follow-up studies, such studies would go a long way toward unpacking the ways in which individuals and groups move through different spaces. It is only through long-term follow-ups that we can begin to understand the interlocking connections between and among race, social class, gender, schooling, and the new economy, engaging theoretical debates in this area and going far beyond what we know to date.

4. Stretching further, we would like to see increased studies of groups similar in race, class, and gender across geographic sites within the Untied States. Michelle Fine and Lois Weis, for example, map experiences and practices since leaving high school among African American, Latino/Latina, and white men and women in the urban Northeast (Fine and Weis, 1998). Based on their data, Fine and Weis come to conclusions regarding the economy, the body politic, and the state. Yet, as Peter McLaren (1997) reminds us, Los Angeles, California, is a wholly different space, no doubt producing different scenarios. And Atlanta, Georgia, has a far more thriving economy than the Northeast, as well as a different kind of racist history. Asking the same kinds of questions in varying geographic contexts within the United States will go a long way toward understanding the relationships between the state and economy and the ways in which individuals and groups forge their lives.

5. Along the lines outlined above, we must also begin to situate our studies globally. Groups can be studied between and among countries such as the United States, Australia, and the United Kingdom, for example, and more time needs to be taken contextualizing what we find within the global economy and meaning systems. In addition, we can usefully explore concepts such as race, for example, by focusing carefully on groups within different national contexts. Nadine Dolby (2001), for one, has begun this work in South Africa, and we encourage others to pursue her agenda.

Final (for Now) Thoughts

The foregoing demands a different set of understandings as to what constitutes what we call the "research imaginary" in education, how we contextualize and understand the lives of urban youths and their connections with educative institutions. Indeed, if we accept a notion of education that implies only traditional school sites and curricula, our work potentially ignores a variety of important complexities in young people's lives—how education happens outside of school, what students bring to the school, and how this intersects with what school offers. At worst, if we uncritically accept a priori parameters for what education "is," we are in danger of simply reproducing the same set of questions, problems, and issues we have inherited. As Jan Nespor writes in *Tangled Up in School: Politics, Space, Bodies, and Signs in the Educational Process (Sociocultural, Political, and Historical Studies in Education)* (1997), "When groups and processes are analytically detached from each other . . . it becomes easy to slide into the bleak loops of contemporary educational debate . . . The debate becomes less simple, but more constructive, when we focus on dense interconnections among various actors and processes" (p. xi).

We have, we argue, an imperative to reimagine our object of study—one that forces us to reengage with the lives of urban youths on fresh terrain, simultaneously challenging predictable notions of culture and identity. This demands cross-site/ cross-space collaborative work in forms in which we have not previously engaged. Evoking recent critical work in geography, we must simultaneously deterritorialize and reterritorialize our objects of study (Helfenbein, 2006). We recall here Michelle Fine's earlier discussion about theoretical generalizability. "To enhance the theoretical generalizability of a study," she writes, "researchers/research collectives might create settings . . . for conversations among researchers, activists, practitioners and theorists who draw from distinct contexts to discuss how, or under what conditions, common and distinct dynamics occur across samples and settings" (2006, p. 99). We look here toward a larger, collective knowledge about how oppression works across disparate sites. Such a discussion should not collapse back into an atomized technical concern with reproducing our findings across multiple, random, and controlled settings. It should spark our imaginations, helping us look outward in hopeful ways—"toward that which is not yet imagined, not yet in practice, not yet in sight" (Fine, 2006, p. 100). We must, then, forge counter-topographies which allow us to think about young people's lives in new and hopeful ways (Katz, 2001). This charge is particularly important in our contemporary moment—a moment in which global capital is aggressively working to structure the lives of the most marginalized and disenfranchised in truly frightening ways. We invite this conversation to continue as we all imagine what research around these issues might look like in the next decade.

I turn now to this short volume's penultimate chapter, as I interrogate the most salient "nodes" for future research in the field.

GLOSSARY

Community-based organizations (CBOs)—out-of-school sites such as community centers or churches where young people choose to spend their free time. Such sites are ideally not bureaucratic institutions as are (typically) traditional schools. They are emergent and unpredictable sites, drawing on the strengths and energies of young people as they work with particular adults, on specific tasks, with real risks and real consequences. CBOs typically offer young people the opportunity to work through real-world activities that demand their full participation.

Multisited ethnography—associated with the work of George Marcus, multisited ethnography means "tracing and describing the connections and relationships among sites previously thought incommensurate" (1998, p. 14). The multisited ethnographer must, in any project, "keep in view and mind two or more ethnographically conceived sites juxtaposed" (p. 4). The multisited ethnographer defines a question and then draws links intuitively across different, tangible sites.

Popular cultures and technologies—the range of affectively charged texts, practices, and technologies young people actively turn to, to make sense out of their lives today.

Research imaginary—the aesthetic space in which we conceive our objects of study or analysis. Through multisited ethnography, for example, we are challenged to imagine our objects of analysis in new and different ways. We are challenged to take responsibility for how we "bound" our object of study.

Safe spaces—term coined by Michelle Fine and Lois Weis for imaginative and literal spaces young people turn to, to "carve out" space for themselves in often oppressive circumstances. These spaces can be in school or out of school, formal or informal—for example, a particularly charged social studies or English class or a Head Start program for young parents or a local arts organization. They are spaces of healing and nurturance where "counterpublics" can be formed—often (ironically) in response to the very exclusionary practices of the public sphere today.

Theoretical generalizability—term coined by Michelle Fine concerned with the ways our research findings and experiences are similar to or different from the findings and experiences of others over time and place. For example, theoretical generalizability might be concerned with two specific ethnographies of youths in poverty in different parts of the world, asking how their experiences are similar or different and why. It is posited in explicit contrast to technical generalizability, which is concerned with the specific replicability of findings in controlled settings.

CHAPTER FOUR

Studying Urban Youth Culture

New Directions

Studying urban youth culture is, of course, a complex affair. As we have seen so far, the language we use is not neutral or value free, nor is the history of the field and the methods being used. They are all packed with often problematic assumptions and connotations, ones we must face up to if we are to advance the field in more ethical ways. In Chapter 3, I (along with Lois Weis) suggested some ways in which we can move this methodological discussion forward in new and perhaps more generative directions—in particular, "denaturalizing" our objects of analysis with new research imaginaries. Grounded in the discussion so far, I look now to chart some of the key substantive issues and concerns facing researchers in the field, suggesting what I see as fruitful areas of inquiry in the years to come. I begin by extending some of the themes and issues raised earlier, detailing how they are now central to thinking through the contemporary terrain of urban youth culture. These include the relationship between culture and structural economic questions in our time of neoliberal retrenchment; the new, emergent redefinition of the suburban and urban and its methodological implications; new forms of identity work in a time of globalization, including the role and importance of youth culture in a "post-subculture" moment; and finally the ethics of studying urban youth, including the new role of youth participatory action research.

Culture and Economics

As noted earlier, work in cultural studies explicitly interrogated and challenged the structural, deterministic focus on class that had dominated much of the work then originating out of the United Kingdom. More specifically, this work opened up a more flexible notion of ideology critique, one that looked at the interpenetrations of "class" and "culture," showing how social actors both resisted and reproduced their class positions in practice. Critical ethnographic traditions in the United States picked up these notions of reproduction and resistance but used them to interrogate a wider range of issues, including race and gender. Of course, these traditions intersected with the legacies of the civil rights and feminist movements that rose to prominence in the United States beginning in the 1960s and 1970s. All this crystallized with what is often called "**multiculturalism**," the popular and academic movement that stressed the interpenetrations of race, class, gender, and other trajectories of inequality that have played out in people's lives.

Multiculturalism
the popular and academic movement that stresses the interpenetrations of race, class, gender, and other trajectories of inequality that play out in people's lives.

This work has continued to inform studies of urban youth culture. In particular, this work has remained largely concerned with the cultural dimensions of young people's lives, how they explore and elaborate upon their creative impulses in often oppressive sets of circumstances. Recall the discussion in Chapter 3 of popular culture and out-of-school learning sites. Yet, to echo my recent work with Lois Weis (this section draws on our recent article in *Teachers College Record* [Weis and Dimitriadis, forthcoming]), we need increasingly to see work on the cultural dimension of urban youths lives in dialogue with the structural, economic issues and pressures that are largely setting youths up for life. In many respects, the impulse to avoid reducing all social phenomena to questions of class, to open up the discussion of difference in complex ways, has served to marginalize such structural, economic issues. This will be an important area of inquiry in years to come. More specifically, we need more studies that look in detail at the ways new economic realities intersect with the quotidian lives of youths.

Work on the economy has taken on a greater urgency of late. In particular, global economic shifts over the past twenty years—marked by the rise of **neoliberalism** and neoliberal logics—have been profound, concentrating increasing amounts of wealth in the hands of very, very few. As Aron-Dine and Shapiro (2006) report, for example, the top 1 percent of households received 53 percent of all income gains in 2004 in the United States. This is the largest such income shift since 1929—a period often referred to as "the Gilded Age." On one level, we see this evidenced in the well-documented move from an industrial to a postindustrial global economy where more and more young people will spend their lives working in service sector jobs that provide minimal income, few if any benefits, and little job security. As is well documented, the vast majority of jobs being created now are not jobs in the so-called **knowledge economy**. Instead, they are low-paying service sector jobs. It is worth recalling that Wal-Mart is the single largest employer in the United States today. On another, broader level, we see this evidenced in the ways that *all* labor is coming to operate under these logics. As Simon Head (2003) points out in *The New Ruthless Economy: Work and Power in the Digital Age*, many of the so-called white-collar job sectors (e.g., those of IT [Information Technology] and health care) have come to "manage" or "reengineer" the work of

---

Neoliberalism
the philosophic belief that unchecked and uncontrolled capitalism is a natural social good.

Knowledge economy
one based on the management of knowledge, intellectual resources, and cognitive skills, not tangible products. The knowledge economy is often posited in explicit contrast to the older industrial economy.

their employees in much the same way that Wal-Mart does—segmenting job tasks into discrete units and "flexibly" farming them out to the cheapest possible workers, whether in the United States or, as is increasingly the case, in nations such as India, Mexico, and China, among others. The net effect has been both the off-shoring of millions and millions of jobs and new, massive concentrations of wealth into fewer hands.

More specifically, as economist Robert Reich (1991, 2001) argues, the U.S. economy shifted away from large-scale production efforts about three decades ago, moving toward modes of "continuous innovation." Such shifts have rapidly—even exponentially—accelerated in recent years. New technologies—technologies of communication, transportation, and information—have widened and deepened the range of consumer choices now available at any moment in time. Consumers now can search for better deals on a range of products and services, forcing parallel pressures on production and competition. "Wider choices and easier switching have intensified competition at all levels—forcing every seller to innovate like mad, cutting costs and adding new value"(Reich, 1991, pp. 106–107). Sellers are thus less secure than ever. "The dynamism and innovation that rewards buyers also subjects sellers to less certainty, more volatility, higher highs and lower lows. Almost all earnings are becoming more volatile, and less predictable" (1991, pp. 106–107). Those at the very top are in the best position to hedge against, help orchestrate, and ultimately benefit from this volatility. The rest of us are left to its mercies—in particular the most vulnerable among us.

In short, the economic context with which youths interact and intersect has changed markedly. For example, if sellers now constantly court buyers through innovation and accompanying cost-cutting mechanisms, this leaves the working class and poor at the mercy of an increasingly competitive yet, in contradictory ways, dynamic economy.

The dynamism that Reich describes renders the working class and poor not superfluous in the sense that they are not needed, but thoroughly economically expendable and/or "exchangeable" given the vagaries of the new business climate: let go when they are not needed or are too expensive, only to be picked up when the next, and highly different, business opportunity comes along. This is strikingly different from dynamics embedded within the old industrial economy, where the "bargain " between capital and labor was such that workers, after much struggle, won a living wage and set of accompanying benefits in return for their labor power. There are no such bargains being struck today, as the global economic context both demands and simultaneously enables the obtaining of wage labor at the lowest level possible, forcing higher and higher numbers of people into sporadic work, no work, or dangerous work such as that associated with the increasingly robust yet simultaneously illegal drug economy in the United States.

In this new, brutal context, the school—in the hard sense of academic attainment and achievement, as measured in particular and intensified ways—has and will continue to become a more pivotal and crucial site of sorting. Quite simply, there is less and less economic room for any "slippage" in the industrialized West in these new global economic circumstances. Although the school has always been a site of sorting through tracking, vocational education versus preparation for college, and so forth, this process now takes a different, more vicious shape and form and is simultaneously more critical in relation to the future trajectories of youth. In other words, the stakes are simply higher—and every parent in America, from the very poor to the upper middle class, knows it. There is ample evidence that schools are becoming an intensified space of sorting, a site that Joel Spring (1989) referred to as the "sorting machine." Although sorting often refers to issues of ability grouping, tracking, and so forth in the academic literature, sorting must be seen as more broadly related to how experiences in schools link to later outcomes.

In sum, we have very little work on how young people's cultural lives intersect and articulate with the pressures of neoliberalism, the new, economic realities that are setting youths up for life. This remains a great challenge to those of us working with urban youths in the new millennium. Even as we look toward and validate the creative practices of youths, we need to understand more specifically how they are negotiating their way—or not—in these new economic times. Even as many of us have looked to the nonformal educative lives of youths— the kinds discussed in the previous chapter—we need to understand more acutely how they come up against global structural economic forces. Part of this project, it seems, would be critically revisiting the long-fashionable notion of "resistance." That is, researchers have long valorized the ways in which young people resist dominant culture and its logics. Yet, we need to understand the long-term implications of such resistance. Willis's lads could often (and often sadly did) move to the shop floor or on to other forms of manual labor. So presumably could Whyte's Norton Boys. But there is little, if any, such work any longer. And the social safety nets long associated with the welfare state are largely eroding in the United States and around the world. We can no longer set up our subjects as mutual foils, root for the resistant underdog, and walk away. At the very least, we have an ethical obligation to see how these resistant practices serve these young people over their life courses. Our economy, I believe, allows for nothing less.

The Urban and Suburban

The so-called New Economy has had attendant effects on the spatial organization of cities, as well— effects that have further complicated the long problematic distinction between the urban and the suburban. This, too, is a fundamental issue and problem that needs revisiting in the next round of scholarship on urban youths. Indeed, as noted earlier, the term "urban" often hides more than it reveals. Invariably posited in stark distinction to the "suburban," it tends to reinforce a classic dichotomy. Whereas the urban is invariably the location of all manner of social pathologies, the suburban is largely marked (or classically unmarked) as a trouble-free zone. This distinction needs to be challenged on several fronts—some empirical, some more symbolic. In either case, the next generation of scholarship on urban youths needs to look toward a new and fresh language—one more in touch and tune with the lived realities of young people.

As Saskia Sassen (2003) has recently noted, so-called new technologies have intersected with new economic pressures to radically reconfigure contemporary notions of urban centers and peripheries. That is to say, with capital free to roam the globe, financial services are coming to concentrate in a select number of cities. Sassen notes that the trend toward the "concentration of top-level management, coordination and servicing functions is evident at the national and international scales in all highly developed countries," highlighting the centrality of cities such as Paris, New York City, London, Zurich, Frankfurt, and Tokyo (p. 216). Other key cities, Joel Kotkin (2006) points out, include Los Angeles, Chicago, Sydney, Toronto, Miami, and Hong Kong. All have fared better than cities that have been left behind in the high-tech revolution—those such as Manchester, Liverpool, Leipzig, Osaka, Turin, Detroit—and, I would add, my own Buffalo (p. 149).

These massive concentrations of wealth have led to new complex relationships between the hyper-wealthy who now live in these cities and the new immigrants, the working class, and other marginalized groups who have traditionally inhabited and worked in them. With rents skyrocketing in massively gentrified (and heretofore heterogeneous) areas such as the Lower East Side in New York City, immigrants, the poor, and the working class often

First-ring suburbs

areas in between dense urban centers and often more affluent outer suburbs or poorer, less densely populated rural areas.

find living arrangements along new peripheries. **First-ring (or inner-ring) suburbs**, for example, are becoming spaces where difference is being fought over and negotiated—more so, in some cases, than in increasingly segregated and gentrified central cities where roles and interactions are largely prescribed and formalized (e.g., between a Starbucks employee and a wealthy businessperson).

All cities, of course, still contain sites of intense poverty and dislocation. Buffalo is a good—if particularly stark—example. The median household income in Buffalo is currently $26,375. The median price of a house is $45,000. Yet, even here, the "urban" and "suburban" dichotomy does not exhaust the discussion of poverty, inequality, and diversity. In fact, as the government report "Poverty in New York State and Buffalo Niagara: Updates from the U.S. Census Bureau" documents, "Over time, the direction of the poverty rate has varied. During the 1990s, poverty fell nationally and in Buffalo Niagara, but increased statewide and in Buffalo Niagara's largest municipalities—including the first-ring suburbs. Since 1999, the trend of rising poverty appears to be continuing in the city and first-ring suburbs. A similar trend is apparent nationally and regionally" (Institute for Local Governance and Regional Growth, 2006, p. 1). The report continues,

> After Amherst, the other large first-ring suburbs— the Towns of Cheektowaga and Tonawanda—both had median household incomes below the U.S. median. Adjusted to 2005 dollars, incomes appear to have eroded across the board—nationally and locally—since 1999, something that afflicted Buffalo and its largest suburbs during the 1990s. If the survey data for 2005 are accurate, the Towns of Amherst and Tonawanda appear to be the hardest hit, which may reflect a real erosion of income, an increase in the population of retired persons, an increase in the non-dormitory college student population, or a combination of these and other factors." (2006, p. 2)

Again, even in a poor city such as Buffalo, we need a more nuanced discussion of the relationship between traditional urban centers and the surrounding suburbs.

No one has been more central in excavating these issues than Myron Orfield (2002). As Orfield writes in his recent *American Metropolitics: The New Suburban Reality* "In region after region, problems associated exclusively with central cities in the national psyche have moved into inner-ring suburbs. . . . Many suburbs have come to recognize that they now have as much, if not more, in common with large cities than their suburban counterparts" (p. 7). He cites several examples. "In Chicago, many south- and west-side suburban districts actually had a higher percentage of blacks and Latinos than the city itself" (p. 14). Even more strikingly, he writes, "Park Forest was the locus of William H. Whyte's *Organization Man,* a classic study of the white collar worker of the 1950s and his suburban life. Today, the schools are increasingly poor and diverse and, per household, the city has a fraction of the local resources of Chicago" (p. 14). He discusses similar trends in Atlanta, Denver, and Minneapolis-St. Paul, among other places.

Again, this points to the ways we need to untangle the traditional isomorphic relationship between space, place, and culture when addressing the needs of disenfranchised youths—a point thrown into sharp relief when we look at this distinction from a global perspective. I recall another example here—this one from Toronto. As Carl James and Roger Saul (forthcoming) recently argued, "[T]oday's immigrants are not living their lives in the traditional reception, or 'inner city' areas of Toronto, Montreal, Calgary, and Vancouver where earlier immigrants tended to settle" (p. 1). In their work, James and Saul draw a very helpful distinction between "inner" and "outer" suburbs. Although the latter remain largely affluent areas, the former are new sites of difference and contestation. They note, "We use the term 'inner-suburban' to refer to the geographic areas outside of the urban core (or inner city), but within the city limits of large Canadian cities that are populated by poor and low income racial minority immigrants" (p. 2). Moreover, the so-called outer-suburban areas can also contain enclaves of immigrant and minority groups (e.g., Asian and South East Asian) who have achieved some degree of social mobility but still challenge long-standing notions of perfectly homogeneous suburban contexts. All of this, again, complicates simple notions of "the urban" in a global context.

Moving beyond simple dichotomous language of "urban" and "suburban" might allow us, I argue, to look at the lives of disenfranchised youths in a global context, in more nuanced and complex ways. I recall here the widely reported, globally transmitted 2005 riots of largely unemployed, minority youths in France. Propelled by the electrocution deaths of two Malian and Tunisian youths as they fled the police in the Parisian suburb of Clichy-sous-Bois, violent protests spread all around the outskirts of Paris—the so-called *banlieue* (outskirts). What was striking to many outside of France is the fact that unlike the Los Angeles, California, riots of a decade earlier, these riots did not unfold in traditional urban centers. Instead, they took place outside Paris, in largely impoverished and underdeveloped, low-income housing areas where many North African youths live. These were the neighborhoods and areas immortalized in Mathieu Kassovitz's 1995 hip-hop fueled film *La Haine* (*The Hate*)—a film that documented the life and culture of *banlieue* youths. The film highlighted the diversity of the *banlieue*—the main characters are Jewish, African, and Arabic—as well as their contentious relationship with the police. When media reports translated *banlieue* as "suburb," or "ghetto suburb," the particular geographic resonance of the term needed to be explained—a telling cross-cultural elision.

The stakes are high here. For too long, the term "urban" has taken on broad symbolic valence, in ways that tend to both reify the lives of young people in particular geographic locales and leave the so-called suburbs as unmarked spaces. A body of work exploring the lives of young people, disenfranchised youths, as they traverse a range of such geographic sites might give us a more precise language here—one that moves us beyond this problematic dichotomy.

Youth Culture, Postsubculture

In the past, youth culture tended to be marked by big, often competing and distinctly marked, cultural movements. For example, rock and roll, disco, punk, hip-hop, and grunge were all popular genres that encompassed a range of music, fashion, dance, and other styles. These were by no means coherent genres, but they did represent a set of practices that had some broad homologies between and among them. Today, the scene is different in some ways. The global proliferation of contemporary media forms has allowed young people to tailor their own leisure practices in very specific and particular ways. If the dominant media model used to be "broadcasting," today's world of inexpensive cable and widespread Internet penetration is perhaps one of "narrowcasting." Young people around the world are carving out new, unpredictable, and in some ways rhizomatic forms of cultural identification in ways often invisible (and typically inexplicable) to adults. Sometimes these forms are defined by taste. Sometimes they are defined by race or ethnic identity. Sometimes—often—they are marked by both.

Inextricably intertwined with this is the emergence of what Henry Jenkins calls "**convergence culture**." Here, Jenkins refers to "the flow of content across multiple media platforms, the cooperation between multiple media industries, the search for new media financing that fall at the interstices between old and new media, and the migratory behavior of media audiences who would go almost anywhere in search of the kind of entertainment experiences they want" (2006, p. 282). If the media

Convergence culture
the new ways in which media content moves across different platforms.

landscape used to be divided fairly clearly between the producers and consumers of popular culture, young people today occupy a new middle ground. Using largely inexpensive forms of technology, young people are creating their own self-styled cultural texts across multiple platforms—as evidenced by the explosion of MySpace, You Tube, Facebook, Blogger, and other such sites. These texts are both proliferating in their own specific communities and speaking back to corporate culture in ways that can have constitutive effects on the material production of culture. The new corporate attention being paid to Internet fan sites and particular bloggers such as Harry Knowles is only one of the many new such phenomena Jenkins highlights.

Cultural studies provided the earliest and in many ways most durable set of tools for understanding youth culture in its full complexity. This work, of course, remains quite valuable. But many of its defining constructs are proving insufficient to address the specificities of our moment (Huq, 2007). Anita Harris (forthcoming) sums this up nicely in her collection *Next Wave Cultures: Feminism, Subcultures, Activism:*

> Nowadays, subcultures are not perceived simply as singular, fixed categories that youth are affiliated to in order to work out their class identities or to resist dominant culture. Instead, theorists talk about neotribes, youth lifestyles, scenes, new communities and so on as momentary and changeable expressions of identity. (p. 3)

The chapters in this collection evidence this complexity associated with what is often called "**postsubculture** studies." We see young women taking on and working through a plethora of cultural practices often associated with men—"gangsterism" and surfing, for example. We see young women carving out safe spaces in subtle and unpredictable ways, around issues such as disability, technology, and religion. We see, finally, a range of ways civic engagement can happen through music, zine writing, street art, and other practices.

Postsubcultures
an empirical and methodological move away from the tightly bounded concept of subcultures.

Subculture theory assumed that groups had stable boundaries that could be explained in terms of both their resistance to and incorporation into an industrial economy. With the rise of postindustrial, neoliberal economic regimes and the destabilizing cultural effects of globalization, however, much more is up for grabs today, as evidenced by this and related works.

Indeed, the shifts and dislocations associated with globalization are registering for young people in often disorientating and paradoxical ways. This is, of course, entirely evident in contemporary youth culture, as discussed in part in the previous chapter. Young people are growing up in a world increasingly marked by new, massive disparities in wealth, the worldwide circulation of (often rigidly fundamentalist) ideologies and belief systems, a dizzying array of signs and symbolic resources dislodged from their traditional moorings, and a veritable explosion of new technologies. Youths are now trying to find their place(s) in this world, moving across this terrain in ways we are only beginning to understand and appreciate. As recent work is making clear, young people are crafting new identities and social networks using a range of globally generated and proliferating resources. Young people are moving, both literally and figuratively, crossing national borders with their bodies as well as imaginations, crafting new and unexpected kinds of identities.

Detailed studies of urban youth culture—studies that move in new theoretical as well as methodological directions—are critical. Toward this end, we have studies such as the aforementioned ones by Dolby (2001) and Yon (2000). These studies highlight the ways in which "urban" cultural texts are circulating around the world, landing in particular ways in particular contexts, in ways that allow youths to articulate their own contemporary circumstances. I recall here, as well, the work of Brett Lashua (2005). For several years, Lashua worked with First Nations youths in the city of Edmonton, Alberta, Canada, helping to construct a studio for these youths to record their own rap songs. As Lashua demonstrated, these young people drew on the dominant tropes and themes in rap music while linking them to the specificity of life on "the rez" (the reservation). Like Dolby and Yon, Lashua shows how these young people address their concerns through contemporary "urban" art forms such as hip-hop. Linked closely to notions of place, these texts have traveled the world, allowing young people to carve out their own senses of self in often hostile sets of social circumstances. Lashua's study throws these issues into sharp relief—highlighting the ways First Nations youths bring their concerns into the urban present through hip-hop, challenging often debilitating stereotypes about indigenous youths.

Such studies blur the line between the production and reception of popular culture. This generative space is one worked well by Leif Gustavson in his important book *Youth Learning on Their Own Terms* (2007). In this powerful text, Gustavson carefully traces the out-of-school creative practices of three youths around the urban East—Ian, Miguel, and Gil—immersing himself in their complex and multifaceted life-worlds, teasing out how they understand the particulars of their crafts. In looking at these creative practices through three very specific biographies, Gustavson highlights their deep and often ignored cognitive components and dimensions. In each of these cases—Ian's zine writing and slam poetry, Miguel's graffiti writing, and Gil's turntable work—we see creative minds at work, making choices and decisions as they work through the intricacies of their media. We see, as well, the particular, productive intersections between these practices and their specific raced and classed backgrounds—not as determining but as constitutive of their material and aesthetic lives.

Benefiting from the theoretical and methodological advances of the past decade, work on contemporary youth culture is moving in several directions at once, opening up multiple and complex notions of identity as it is lived in the everyday. In particular, this work looks toward the ways in which young people are navigating their everyday lives using popular cultural texts—including the ones marked as "urban"—in complex and unpredictable ways. None of this work reduces the lives and experiences of these youths to tight subcultural boundaries.

Ethics Today

Finally, qualitative researchers today are facing new ethical demands from nearly every direction and quarter. As noted throughout this book, the notion of the disinterested, neutral observer has been called inextricably into question, forcing researchers to take new kinds of responsibilities for their work, both in the field and at the desk. Although ethnographies of urban youths have historically been marked by political uplift agendas, the so-called critical turn has been marked by more explicitly ontological concerns. I would like to briefly explore one such response to this moment—**youth participatory action research (YPAR)**.

Youth participatory action research (YPAR)

the notion that research should be conducted collaboratively with youths—not on them.

YPAR is a particular method of working with youths, but it also reflects a more basic set of assumptions about how knowledge is produced and created. As Tuck and Fine (2007) write, YPAR has the following characteristics: "the design is collaboratively negotiated and co-constructed; research questions are co-constructed; there is a transparency on all matters of the research, from administrative details like institutional review board approval to the budget to the theory and reasoning behind practice; analysis is co-constructed; research projects are collaboratively drafted" (p. 165). A recent collection, *Revolutionizing Education: Youth Participatory Action Research in Education* (Cammarota and Fine, forthcoming) brings together many important such projects, examples of researchers (particularly and markedly "junior" ones) working with youths around key issues—Torre and Fine on the *Brown v. Board of Education* decision and its legacies, Tuck and colleagues on the role and importance of the Graduate Record Examination as a credential, Cahill and colleges on the gentrification of New York City neighborhoods, Romero and colleagues on a social science curriculum designed to empower Latin youths around issues of educational segregation, and Morrell and colleagues on a summer Youth Summit in Los Angeles, California, designed to bring together stakeholders on race and class inequalities. As the editors sum up in the book's introduction,

> YPAR represents a systematic approach for engaging young people in transformational resistance, educational praxis, and critical epistemologies. By attaining knowledge for resistance and transformation, young people create their own sense of efficacy in the world and address the social conditions that impede liberation and positive, healthy development. Learning to act upon and address oppressive social conditions leads to the acknowledgement of one's ability to reshape the context of one's life and thus determine a proactive and empowered sense of self. (p. xx)

YPAR underscores and is one response to an important debate recently opened up by Arjun Appadurai—one well worth attending to as this book moves toward a conclusion. As Appadurai (2006) recently argued, the ability to conduct research on one's social surrounding should be considered a basic human right. By "the right to research," Appadurai means "the right to the tools through which any citizen can systematically increase that stock of knowledge which they consider most vital to their survival as human beings and to their claims as citizens" (p. 168). In positing research as a human right—and I believe it is—Appadurai works toward two self-professed and interconnected goals. The first is substantive. Full citizenship today demands the ability to make "strategic" and "continuous" inquiries on a range of issues—AIDS, riots, labor market shifts, migration paths, and prisons, among them (p. 168). Clearly, while neoliberal logics continue to unfold around the world, they land in unpredictable ways in particular communities. Critically interrogating key issues with youths allows us sharper perspective on them—allows us to see that they can be otherwise. This is a capacity often denied youths, although it is necessary for a vibrant public sphere—for a democracy (to echo Michael Apple, a leading critical educational theorist) worth its name.

The second goal is what Appadurai calls "rhetorical." By opening up the notion of "research," we "de-parochialize" it, taking these tools out of the hands of an elite group of specialists and professionals, making it a "much more universal, elementary and improvable capacity" (p. 168). We need to extend the notion of the so-called expert to encompass a wider range of stakeholders. At its very best, such work opens up a space for a critical multigenerational dialogue about research itself—one that looks beyond rarified university walls. This is a fundamental challenge to the ways research is traditionally conducted and knowledge is traditionally stratified. It too is necessary for universities to meaningfully engage in democratic dialogue in these new and uncertain times.

None of this is easy work. Such work forces us to abandon the categories often used to sort, classify, and essentialize youths. These categories can be deployed by both conservatives and progressives. The former often treat young people as a pathological problem to be managed—"at risk" as defined by adults. The latter often treat young people as incipient radicals, "resisting" dominant culture through everyday cultural practices. Working with youths, in distinction, means seeing young people as partners in struggle, as resources to be drawn upon in common cause.

Final Thought

As evidenced throughout this book so far, qualitative research on urban youth culture today moves in the interstices between pedagogy, research, and politics.

Yet each does not extend from the others in seamless fashion. Each demands specific competencies and skills, both on their own and taken together. If nothing else, this is an invitation to a long-term struggle that forces us to operate in such in-between spaces. This is a site of intense possibility as well as uncertainty. It is one best seen in its specificity and detail, as I hope I have demonstrated throughout. At stake here is what Appadurai calls the "capacity to aspire," the capacity to imaginatively link one's own personal problems and issues to a broader set of social, political, and economic forces and pressures—and to work to transform them (2006, p. 176).

We turn now to the book's final chapter—a chapter that discusses the practical and conceptual methodological strategies often deployed to study urban youths. This discussion hopefully brings this volume's discussion closer to the ground.

GLOSSARY

Convergence culture—the new ways in which media content moves across different platforms—for example, across the Internet to film or videogames and back again. Convergence culture cuts across the old distinction between the "producers" and "consumers" of popular culture. It highlights, for example, the ways in which young people are using largely inexpensive technology to create their own self-styled content across multiple platforms. This is evidenced by the explosion of MySpace, YouTube, Facebook, Blogger, and other such sites.

First-ring suburbs—areas in between dense urban centers and often more affluent outer suburbs or poorer, less densely populated rural areas. First-ring suburbs are often new sites of national migration and international immigration. First-ring suburbs are increasingly heterogeneous places, often marked by the poverty and disaffection usually associated with urban areas.

Knowledge economy—one based on the management of knowledge, intellectual resources, and cognitive skills, not tangible products. The knowledge economy is often posited in explicit contrast to the older industrial economy. It is often linked to the belief that we live in a globally interconnected, high-tech, and information-rich society.

Multiculturalism—the popular and academic movement that stresses the interpenetrations of race, class, gender, and other trajectories of inequality that play out in people's lives.

Neoliberalism—often referred to as capitalism "without the gloves on." That is, neoliberalism is the philosophic belief that unchecked and uncontrolled capitalism is a natural social good. Neoliberalism represents the triumph of the global marketplace over any other kind of moral or ethical discourse. Neoliberalism has also been associated with the withering of the public sphere and its safety nets and supports.

Postsubcultures—an empirical and methodological move away from the tightly bounded concept of subcultures. As Anita Harris (forthcoming) writes, "Nowadays, subcultures are not perceived simply as singular, fixed categories that youth are affiliated to in order to work out their class identities or to resist dominant culture. Instead, theorists talk about neotribes, youth lifestyles, scenes, new communities, and so on as momentary and changeable expressions of identity."

Youth participatory action research (YPAR)—the notion that research should be conducted with youth—not on them. As Tuck and Fine (2007) write, YPAR has the following characteristics: "the design is collaboratively negotiated and co-constructed; research questions are co-constructed; there is a transparency on all matters of the research, from administrative details like institutional review board approval to the budget to the theory and reasoning behind practice; analysis is co-constructed; research projects are collaboratively drafted" (p. 165).

Looking Toward the Past and the Future

Making Methods

In this final chapter, I look simultaneously toward the past and the future of qualitative methods, both in the field and at the desk. In closing with this chapter, I look outward with the reader toward the kinds of methods we may deploy when taking on the types of practical and theoretical questions raised throughout the book. This chapter, I hope, will land this book squarely in the everyday and practical realities of studying urban youth culture. This discussion compresses a wide range of material. Further readings will be suggested in key areas. I open up a discussion here about how researchers construct questions about urban youth culture, the particular techniques of data collection often associated with qualitative inquiry (one-on-one interviews, focus groups, and participant-observation, among them), and, finally, the interpretation and writing process itself. This chapter will attempt to unpack many of the technical aspects to qualitative research, technical discussions often "written out" of major texts such as the ones discussed in Chapter 2.

I begin by disentangling four distinct constructions—epistemologies, theories, approaches, and strategies (such as those mentioned above). Although many research texts conflate these, they are actually very distinct constructions (Kamberelis and Dimitriadis, 2005, pp. 13–20). **Epistemologies** are concerned with the question of knowledge and how people come to possess it (e.g., does one have an objectivist or interpretive understanding of the world?). **Theories** are abstract sets of assumptions and assertions used to interpret, understand, and act upon individual, social, and cultural processes and dynamics (e.g., is one a Marxist, feminist, and/or post-structuralist?). Next, **approaches** are formations that provide loosely defined structures for conceiving, designing, and carrying out research projects (e.g., does one do ethnography, life history, and/or grounded theory studies?). Finally, **strategies** are methods or techniques used to collect and analyze empirical material (e.g., does one use interviews, observations, or archival data?). Most of this chapter focuses on the last construct—the practical "strategies" researchers use. Again, each of these constructs is distinct. Each has its own autonomy and integrity. None can be mapped, necessarily, on to another in unproblematic ways.

Perhaps an example might help. Theorists and researchers such as Pierre Bourdieu (1983) have used quantitative methods while holding on to a fundamentally critical and interpretive epistemology. *Distinction* (1984), for example, employs a wide range of methods, including large-scale surveys and statistical analyses. Yet Bourdieu needed a range of research techniques typically associated with qualitative research, including in-depth narrative accounts, to make sense out of his quantitative surveys. His goal in this book was to show how "taste" is linked to the reproduction of social class. This is a fundamentally critical and interpretive gesture. As numbers are simply another way of representing

---

Epistemologies

concerned with the question of knowledge and how people come to possess it. For example, does one have an objectivist or interpretive understanding of the world?

Theories

abstract sets of assumptions and assertions used to interpret, understand, and act upon individual, social, and cultural processes and dynamics.

Approaches

formations that provide loosely defined structures for conceiving, designing, and carrying out research projects.

Strategies

methods or techniques used to collect and analyze empirical material.

reality, Bourdieu's use of quantifiable data highlights the fallacy of stark splits between what we call "qualitative" and "quantitative" empirical material. Kamberelis and I (2005) sum up, "Qualitative researchers often quantify social action as part of their interpretive work, and the results of statistical analysis require interpretation" (p. 22). Yet there has tended to be an unfortunate conflation of epistemological and methodological concerns in both the literature and received wisdom on research. That is, the assumption is often that those with an interpretive orientation use qualitative research methods, while those with a positivist orientation use quantitative methods. Even as this volume has focused on qualitative research, it is important to note that this is a false and highly debilitating dichotomy.

Constructing a Question

Research question

the overarching guiding question one has about a particular social phenomenon or body of theory or literature.

Constructing a guiding **research question** is both a deeply ethical and deeply aesthetic undertaking (Marshall and Rossman, 1995). As Foucault so famously noted, the proliferation of particular discourses is a function of power itself. One does not simply ask "neutral" questions. By asking one question and not another, one problematizes a certain issue. Take for example, as in Chapter 2, the continual focus on young black men in the history of the literature on urban youth. Although often attempting to address real questions and problems and often quite self-conscious about the limits of such work, this focus has continued to construct young black men as "the problem." There is no comparable body of work on white urban youth. There is certainly no similar body of work that focuses on youth culture in suburban settings. Importantly, constructing research problems often seems like a neutral and even inevitable endeavor—that, in fact, is often their power. But, as we saw, this focus on black youth was not always defined in the field. In fact, the earliest studies focused on ethnic and not racial minorities. Again, undertaking any research project or question means both proliferating and potentially disrupting a particular body of knowledge. This is a deeply ethical endeavor.

Constructing a guiding research question is also a deeply aesthetic endeavor. That is, orchestrating a question often means engaging with distinct bodies of literature in new and creative ways, weaving them together in ways that open up spaces for particular projects. This "work" is often done in the so-called **literature review** section of articles and books. This is not the place to discuss the technicalities of writing such reviews (see Hart, 1999). Instead, I highlight the often recursive and creative nature of this project. Whereas literature reviews often unfold in a linear fashion, giving the impression of a curious and disinterested scholar who simply identifies a "gap" in the literature and aims to fill it, the reality is often more messy. Constructing a researchable question is in many ways the most difficult and nuanced part of any research project. When studying urban youth, one can seemingly begin from several different points. One can observe a real-world phenomenon that has heretofore not been examined in great detail or depth. One can begin by addressing a substantive "gap" in extant academic literature. Finally, one can look to extend or deepen an extant body of work. Often these three approaches, in reality, blend together in complex ways.

Let's take the case of hip-hop and urban youth and think through some possible studies. For example, I suggest the aforementioned phenomenon offered by Bakari Kitwana (2005)—that is, young middle-class female fans of white hip-hop artist Eminem traveling from a Cleveland suburb to attend a concert in Detroit (an interesting and unique population). Such a study might look at how these fans talk about the role and importance of Eminem in their lives. Such a study would be interesting for several reasons. It would explore the phenomenon of suburban young adults drawn to hip-hop—in particular young women. Hip-hop is often assumed to be the purview of young

Literature review
the section of a research report or book that describes how others have written about one's particular object of analysis.

black teens. Such a study would challenge those assumptions, opening up the cultural dimensions of urban culture in interesting and important ways. Moreover, such a study would help explain the phenomenon of white rapper Eminem, who has been unique among white rappers in crossing over to a black audience. In many respects, his career has been a complex and certainly interesting one for understanding the fluidity of race and popular culture today. This study would usefully explore the lives and experiences of these women and their particular relationship to Eminem. It would contribute usefully to the body of work on hip-hop, urban youth, and race in the United States most broadly.

Another example might be the gap in the literature to date on the production of commercial hip-hop recordings. There is a wide range of scholarship on hip-hop—scholarship perhaps best summed up in the 2004 collection *That's the Joint! The Hip-Hop Studies Reader* (Forman and Neal, 2004). This volume is replete with different approaches to hip-hop—approaches that have explored hip-hop socially, historically, culturally, and theoretically. Yet virtually all of these chapters take hip-hop texts themselves as given, circulating artifacts. One has very little sense in this work or in other work on hip-hop of exactly how these texts are produced—that is, the complex process an amateur artist goes through in becoming a commercial rapper, his or her interactions with a commercial recording company and their particular demands and needs, the production and recording process, as well as the final dissemination and promotion of a product. Although there have been popular and anecdotal accounts of this trajectory or arc, one wonders what a more formal, qualitative research study would reveal about this process. All or part of this would be a very valuable contribution to the academic literature on hip-hop. To undertake such a study, one would need to find ways to gain access, a research site, and the like. This would be an example of a question that begins as an intervention in the literature.

As a final example, I suggest the small body of empirical work on hip-hop and globalization. This work has looked at the particular ways in which hip-hop music and culture has landed in specific ways around the world. For example, there has been important work on hip-hop in Japan— Ian Condry's *Hip-Hop Japan: Rap and the Paths of Cultural Globalization* (2006), Tony Mitchell's *Global Noise: Rap and Hip-Hop outside of the USA* (2001), and Rupa Huq's *Beyond Subculture: Pop, Youth, and Identity in a Postcolonial World* (2006). In addition, several recent dissertations have looked at hip-hop in global contexts such as among indigenous youth in Edmonton, Alberta, Canada (Lashua, 2005) as well as Berlin, Germany (Templeton, 2006). Indeed, as hip-hop has circulated globally, young people have picked up and "used" these texts in ways that address their local circumstances. This has led to a particular confluence of the local and the global in ways we are only beginning to understand. But there is clearly more room for such studies in other contexts around the world as well as in the United States. (In fact, there has been comparatively little empirical work on hip-hop in the United States.) All this underscores how studies of urban youth culture can extend extant work in important ways.

In sum, there are different ways in which one can embark on a research project. These are only examples of approaches related to one particular issue. Importantly, each of these questions presupposes an engagement with extant literature in the field—here, hip-hop (specifically) and urban youth culture (more broadly). Moreover, each of these questions presupposes a different, specific body of work—the first, on whiteness and gender, the second, on musicology and institutional analysis, and the third, on globalization. All of this underscores the importance of reading to the process of both formulating questions and situating one's work within ongoing dialogues. I suggest here that it is impossible to separate out the processes of reading, writing, and researching issues

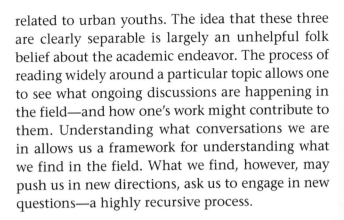

related to urban youths. The idea that these three are clearly separable is largely an unhelpful folk belief about the academic endeavor. The process of reading widely around a particular topic allows one to see what ongoing discussions are happening in the field—and how one's work might contribute to them. Understanding what conversations we are in allows us a framework for understanding what we find in the field. What we find, however, may push us in new directions, ask us to engage in new questions—a highly recursive process.

Strategies

I now discuss the different research techniques most often used to study urban youths, situating them both conceptually and practically.

From Observation to Participant-Observation

Participant-observation
method in which researchers spend long stretches of time with social actors in specific naturalistic contexts as a way to investigate, document, and experience ongoing social action.

The earliest anthropologists and sociologists used observation and **participant-observation** (more on this distinction in a moment) in conducting their classic ethnographies. From *The Gang: A Study of 1,313 Gangs in Chicago* (Thrasher, 1927) to *Framing Dropouts: Notes on the Politics of an Urban Public High School* (Fine, 1991), researchers have relied on what is often called (sometimes pejoratively) "deep hanging out" to understand the flux and flow of social action in context. Sometimes this kind of work is carried out in a broad geographic area (as Thrasher's book) or a more bounded site (as in Fine's). In all these cases, researchers spend long stretches of time with social actors in specific, naturalistic contexts as a way to investigate, document, and experience ongoing social action. As opposed to formal interviews, this method allows the researcher to engage participants on unfamiliar terrain, fostering new kinds of understandings about how people give meaning to their lives, experiences, and events. This distinction between "observer" and "participant" is worth underscoring. Each can be usefully thought of as a point on a continuum. Traditionally, the former has been associated with detachment from ongoing social action. For example, many of the most important ethnographies of urban school settings have used classroom observation as a key method. The researcher will try to be as unobtrusive as possible here, often taking detailed fieldnotes of classroom interaction from the back of the room. Traditionally, the latter has been associated with a more active involvement or participation in ongoing social action. For example, many of these same studies detail the informal interactions among students and between students and staff. The researcher, here, might eat with students in the cafeteria or accompany them after school to do what they do as they do it.

Thus, the researcher can move across this continuum—from observation to participation. Most often, this method is called "participant-observation," with the understanding that one typically takes on different roles at different times in the fieldwork process. This method has been especially useful for understanding events in deep, holistic context—events often difficult if not impossible to understand from a distance. This is a particularly salient concern for studying urban youth culture. For example, Philippe Bourgois's *In Search of Respect: Selling Crack in El Barrio* (1995) is a five-year study of street-level drug dealers in East Harlem, New York City. Such a study necessitated a deep immersion in the life-world of these young men, gaining their trust, getting beyond the "rhetoric" that often surrounds drug dealing, giving the reader a much deeper understanding of the logic of their choices and life courses in radical, local context. Bourgois begins the book by discussing how traditional survey analysis could not hope to get at the realities of street-level drug dealers. He notes that "traditional social science research techniques that rely on Census Bureau statistics or random sample neighborhood surveys cannot access with any degree of accuracy the people who survive in the underground economy—and much less those who sell or take illegal drugs" (p. 12). The point is self-evident in many ways—people engaging in illegal activities will often misrepresent their behaviors to others—particularly to those in authoritative positions.

Instead, Bourgois deployed the tools of participant-observation, spending countless hours on the streets and in crack houses, observing dealers and addicts, often tape-recording conversations, interviews, and life-history narratives. He also talks of visiting the biological and extended families of the men with whom he worked—attending Thanksgiving dinners and New Year's Eve celebrations—often interviewing these people as well (p. 13). Such an approach gives us a stunningly rich—singular, in many ways—insight into the lives and experiences of these men. Such an approach gets us beyond the deadening and often highly deceptive quantitative data generated about drug dealing. He writes of his methodological approach,

> The participant-observation techniques developed primarily by cultural anthropologists since the 1920s are better suited than exclusively quantitative methodologies for documenting the lives of people who live on the margins of a society that is hostile to them. Only by establishing long-term relationships based on trust can one begin to ask provocative personal questions, and expect thoughtful, serious answers. Ethnographers usually live in the communities they study, and they establish long-term, organic relationships with the people they write about. In other words, to collect "accurate data," ethnographers violate the canons of positivist research: we become intimately involved with the people we study. (p. 13)

Bourgois underscores the importance of this particular methodology—particularly for studying disenfranchised or marginalized groups. He also raises the complex question of the relationship between observation and interview data and the so-called "veracity" of the latter versus the former. This is an issue I take up later.

For now, I would like to underscore the power of participant-observation as a methodology for studying urban youths (see also Nightingale, 1995). I highlight a tension inherent in this methodological approach—what Atkinson, Coffey, and Delamont (2003) call the tension between "strangeness" and "familiarity" in qualitative research. As these authors make clear, the earliest impulses in qualitative research were to make the familiar strange. That is to say, the researcher's impulse was to immerse him or herself in an unfamiliar set of circumstances, to "resocialize" him or herself in a distinct and different set of contexts. Indeed, anthropologists long compared the researcher in the field to a child—someone who has to learn rules and mores from the ground up. Outsiders can often see what is blindingly routinized to insiders as marked. This, again, is one of the most powerful tools for studying urban youths. Yet, as the authors note, this impulse to see the familiar as strange can also exoticize our research subjects. This is particularly a problem considering that so much of the work to date on urban youths has constructed them as the "other." This is a complex matter, as there is the parallel danger of seeing the world through overly familiar sets of lenses. They note,

> "Othering"—in the sense of treating cultures and social groups as inherently exotic and alien—is no longer acceptable, intellectually and morally. On the other hand, we still need to recognize that the purpose of ethnographic field research is to make sense of social settings we are not familiar with, and to make strange social contexts that we assume we understand by virtue of our taken-for-granted cultural competence. (p. 47)

As several recent texts point out, such work can be carried on in a practical and efficacious way. In particular, the book *Writing Ethnographic Fieldnotes* (1995) by Emerson, Fretz, and Shaw underscores the power of this methodology as well as its literary dimensions. Indeed, fieldworkers understand their experiences in the field largely through writing rigorous **ethnographic fieldnotes**. These fieldnotes are the primary records researchers have of their experiences. Inscribing such notes is a deeply

Fieldnotes
the primary records researchers keep of their experiences in the field.

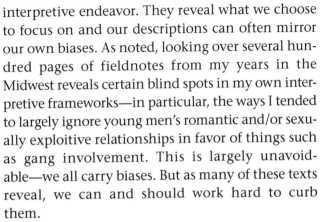

interpretive endeavor. They reveal what we choose to focus on and our descriptions can often mirror our own biases. As noted, looking over several hundred pages of fieldnotes from my years in the Midwest reveals certain blind spots in my own interpretive frameworks—in particular, the ways I tended to largely ignore young men's romantic and/or sexually exploitive relationships in favor of things such as gang involvement. This is largely unavoidable—we all carry biases. But as many of these texts reveal, we can and should work hard to curb them.

The best, most useful fieldnotes attempt to document in detail ongoing social action. They do not move too quickly to interpretation. They record detail—for example, who said what to whom and under (exactly) what circumstances. They do not describe scenes with generic phrases such as "chaotic." They describe what is happening. They do not describe people as character types, such as "controlling." They describe individual action in detail. They do not interpret broad, social processes too quickly with limited data. Nor are they a venue for personal reflection. Instead, these latter two kinds of writing should be kept separate—as analytic memos and reflective notes, respectively. The goal is to acquire as much detailed information as possible. The goal is to describe scenes and episodes, record dialogue, characterize individuals. As the authors write, "Field researchers seek to get close to others in order to understand their ways of life. To preserve and convey that closeness, they must describe situations and events of interest in detail" (p. 14). They continue, "Writing fieldnotes as soon and as fully as possible after events of interest have occurred encourages detailed descriptions of the processes of interaction through which members of social settings create and sustain specific, local realities" (p. 14).

Yet all writing is an interpretive endeavor. Emerson, Fretz, and Shaw (1995) encourage the researcher to treat these notes as a literary endeavor—and writing choices will have implications for the kinds of data one will record. For example, *Writing Ethnographic Fieldnotes* discusses the choices one can make when writing these notes. One can write from multiple points of view—including the first person, the third person, and the omniscient voice. Each has implications for the kinds of information gathered. The first person allows the researcher to explicitly situate his or her observations in concrete and personal ways. The third person allows the researcher a little more discursive distance, allowing the researcher to focus more explicitly on a wider range of social actors in the field. Finally, the omniscient voice allows the researcher wider access to the thoughts, feeling, and emotions of such actors. In many ways, it is the most dangerous of the three stances—it assumes the most—but it can also be quite useful. In addition, one can write notes in real time, that is, as they unfold moment by moment. One can also write from a specific end point—that is, from a retrospective position. The former implies that the importance of events, scenes, and individuals has not yet been sorted—they are unfolding in time. The latter implies that the importance of events, scenes, and individuals has already been sorted—they are being narrated from this point, in retrospect. Finally, the authors caution against creating narrative closure too quickly across fieldnotes—that is, they advise keeping one's notes in sequential order, keeping events and activities separate. A narrative implies an overarching explanation. It can lead to premature "closure" on interpretation.

Interviews
structured, semistructured, or unstructured conversations between researchers and research participants. They can be conducted with single individuals or can be larger group discussions or focus groups.

From In-Depth Interviewing to Focus Groups

Another extremely popular method for studying urban youths is **interviewing**. Interviews can be structured, semistructured, and unstructured. They can be conducted with single individuals or can be larger group discussions or focus groups. Interviewing has become an increasingly popular method for several reasons—some intellectual,

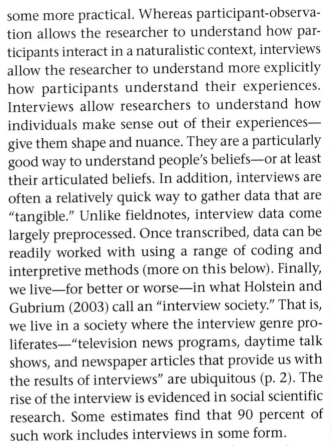

some more practical. Whereas participant-observation allows the researcher to understand how participants interact in a naturalistic context, interviews allow the researcher to understand more explicitly how participants understand their experiences. Interviews allow researchers to understand how individuals make sense out of their experiences—give them shape and nuance. They are a particularly good way to understand people's beliefs—or at least their articulated beliefs. In addition, interviews are often a relatively quick way to gather data that are "tangible." Unlike fieldnotes, interview data come largely preprocessed. Once transcribed, data can be readily worked with using a range of coding and interpretive methods (more on this below). Finally, we live—for better or worse—in what Holstein and Gubrium (2003) call an "interview society." That is, we live in a society where the interview genre proliferates—"television news programs, daytime talk shows, and newspaper articles that provide us with the results of interviews" are ubiquitous (p. 2). The rise of the interview is evidenced in social scientific research. Some estimates find that 90 percent of such work includes interviews in some form.

Interviews are sometimes used as a primary research tool in studying urban youths. For example, Catherine Cornbleth's *Hearing American Youth: Social Identities in Uncertain Times* (2003) relied largely on one-on-one interviews with diverse urban youths who were asked to describe or characterize America. More specifically, she writes,

> Our interview question to students was open-ended: In the United States, it is common to identify or describe people according to the groups to which they seem to belong. For example, people talk about racial/ethnic, cultural, national, language, religious, social class, age, gender, and political groups. Which, if any, of these groups—or others—do you use to identify yourself? (p. 11)

The results allowed young people to define themselves outside or beyond the "checklist" approach evidenced on many censuslike forms. It allowed them to express their hopes in and doubts for the so-called American ideal. "What it means to these young people to be an American varies, and numerous students offered more than one meaning" (p. 135). The responses are nuanced and complex. Indeed, this is one of the most powerful aspects to interviewing. It allows, at least in theory, for participants to set the terms upon which they want to define their response. Marshall and Rossman (1995) wrote that "qualitative interviews are much more like conversations than formal events with predetermined response categories. The researcher explores a few general topics to help uncover the participant's meaning perspective but otherwise respects how the participant frames and structures the response" (p. 80). Thus Cornbleth's participants were able to articulate a complex set of responses about their identities that did not fit into neat categories. Again, in-depth interviewing can be a useful tool in projects which study urban youth culture.

Interviews are often used in tandem with participant-observations. As Atkinson, Coffey, and Delamont (2003) note, the relationship between the two has often been posited as a simple dichotomy—we get, respectively, "what people say" and "what people do" through these methods. The latter, of course, is often posited as closer to the truth. The reality, they note, is that each method represents a certain kind of social action that get us different kinds of data that can often be complementary. Interviews allow people to actively construct and perform a certain kind of social self in the interview setting. Participant-observation allows researchers to see this kind of social performance of self in the everyday, in naturalistic contexts. Each can yield useful kinds of data. Taken together, they can allow the researcher different angles of vision on particular phenomena. Indeed, most full-blown ethnographies use both methods. As noted earlier, Philippe Bourgois was able to deploy both methods in complementary ways. Participant-observation allowed him to observe the everyday worlds of street-level drug dealers, building up a fund of knowledge about these activities, as well as the trust of participants. He was then able to flesh out their stories with in-depth interviews, often producing life-history narratives.

Focus groups are larger group conversations. They too can vary in size and can be directed or nondirected. Such groups are often helpful for disrupting the authority of the researcher, allowing participants to take over groups. These can be very helpful for working with disenfranchised groups, including urban youths. For example Esther Madriz (2000) discussed the role and importance of focus groups in her work on young women and perceptions of violence. Much of her discussion focused on political (and politicized) uses of focus groups within qualitative inquiry. As Madriz showed, within feminist and womanist traditions, there is a long history of deploying focus groups in consciousness raising activities and for promoting social justice agendas. "Focus groups, as a form of collective testimony, can become an empowering experience for women in general and for women of color in particular" (p. 843). Madriz argues that focus groups decenter the authority of the researcher, allowing women themselves safe spaces to talk about their own lives and struggles. These groups allow women to connect with each other collectively, to share their own experiences and "reclaim their humanity" in a nurturing context (p. 843). Very often, she notes, women themselves take these groups over, reconceptualizing them in very basic kinds of ways.

There are, clearly, political implications here. She writes, "I argue that focus groups can be an important element in the advancement of an agenda of social justice for women, because they can serve to expose and validate women's everyday experiences of subjugation and their individual and collective survival and resistance strategies" (p. 836). As Madriz notes, these groups allow women space for "testimony," space to find their own "voice." She continues, "Group interviews are particularly suited for uncovering women's daily experience through collective stories and resistance narratives that are filled with cultural symbols, words, signs, and ideological representations that reflect different dimensions of power and domination that frame women's quotidian experiences" (p. 839).

This discussion of testimonies, as well as life histories, more broadly underscores the importance of **narrative** in qualitative interviewing. Narratives are a particularly powerful way in which to understand people's lives and experiences. In her book *Narrative Analysis* (1993), Riessman notes that narrative analysis is a method that underscores several profound questions—why was a story told one way and not another? How do people impose order and make sense out of their lives? For Riessman, language is not a transparent reflection of one's experiences and realities. Exploring narratives places us at the intersection of the humanities and the social sciences. She highlights several models for understanding narratives, including those of William Labov, a linguist. Labov's work in the 1960s and 1970s focused on young black gang members in Harlem, New York—in particular, their stories of street fights. Based on his analysis of these stories, Labov (1972) proposed a six-part structure for any "fully formed narrative." These elements of narrative have since become commonplace to many scholars of narratives and their functions. According to Labov, a fully formed narrative has an abstract (which summarizes the story), an orientation (which introduces the parties, place, and time relevant to the story), at least one complicating action (what happened to mark these events as special), an evaluation (the way the speaker responded to the complicating action), a resolution (what finally happened), and a coda (which returns the speaker to the present) (pp. 362–396). Hence, Labov's narrator represents some past action in a particular way, presenting himself or herself as actively evaluating and responding to a particular situation in a particular way. The work of language is thus central

Narratives
typically first-person stories people tell about particular incidents, events, and people.

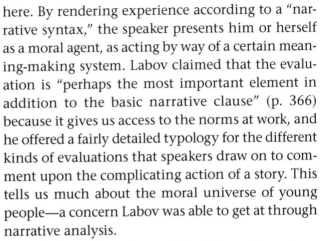

here. By rendering experience according to a "narrative syntax," the speaker presents him or herself as a moral agent, as acting by way of a certain meaning-making system. Labov claimed that the evaluation is "perhaps the most important element in addition to the basic narrative clause" (p. 366) because it gives us access to the norms at work, and he offered a fairly detailed typology for the different kinds of evaluations that speakers draw on to comment upon the complicating action of a story. This tells us much about the moral universe of young people—a concern Labov was able to get at through narrative analysis.

Riessman also points out the interpretive nature of the transcription process—one more place where we are called upon to transform experience. Here, the researcher must transform aurally recorded words into written text. As Blake Poland (2003) points out, transcription is often assumed to be a purely neutral functional endeavor. But there are all kinds of decisions we must make along the way. Such decisions include how we choose to punctuate people's words (people don't speak, of course, with commas and periods, nor do they break their sentences into paragraphs); if and how we represent silence, increases and decreases in volume, stress on particular words, and other paralinguistic cues; and how we choose to clean up or not the words of our participants (editing out grammatical errors, omitting words such as "um" and phrases such as "you know"). These are all interpretive decisions, often with ethnical implications. For example, does cleaning up the grammar of urban youths rob them of their own language and its specificity? Or do we present their words as spoken and risk making them appear ignorant? What does the move to text demand of us?

Finally, as with work on participant-observation, there are particular strategies for eliciting rich data. Although this is not the place for an elaborated discussion, Irving Seidman's *Interviewing As Qualitative Research* (2006) provides several such tips. These include asking open-ended questions. That is, ask questions that leave room for participants to open up and move in several directions at once. Thus ,one might ask the young suburban women in the first example, "What does Eminem mean to you?" He then advises listening more and talking less, following up on what people say. "Tell me more about . . ." is always a good way to keep a discussion going. In addition, it is always best to formulate questions that can best elicit concrete detail. For example, a vague question might be "Besides Eminem, what other kinds of music do you like?" A better question might be "Besides Eminem, what are the last 5 CDs you bought?" It is always good to get people to tell stories. Again, a productive question might be "Tell me about your last 'road trip' to see Eminem." The goal is, always, to get to the rich and complex details that give us insight into people's lives.

At the Desk

As noted above, the writing process was called inextricably into question by the "writing culture" movement of the mid-1980s. The movement underscored the ways in which bodies of expert knowledge are produced and disseminated, creating "neat fictions" that serve to create particular notions of the "other." Although Clifford (1997) and others were anthropologists and focused largely on cultures outside the United States, the work has clear implications for our understandings of urban youths. Indeed, when writing about urban youths, we need to be acutely aware of the ways in which these youths have been discursively "framed" in the popular imagination. As Norman Denzin (2002) pointed out, for example, the debilitating frameworks provided in film and other popular media have largely defined and limited the discussion of race in the United States. For Denzin, social scientists have traditionally worked in sync with these popular images, reinforcing them in their work. This all makes the process of writing up our contrary and critical stories about urban youths a deeply ethical process.

Grounded theory
the impulse to build ground-up theories about social phenomena from extant data.

There are many different methods for interpreting fieldnotes and interview transcripts. One most commonly referenced is **grounded theory**. Emerging from a modernist effort to create a harder "science" out of qualitative research (Denzin and Lincoln, 2005), grounded theory is the impulse to build ground-up theories about social phenomena from extant data. Typically, this method entails coding one's data—first, open coding and, second, focused coding. One begins by applying short descriptive codes to particular short chunks of data. This is done in a fairly open-ended fashion. One then looks across these codes to see whether there is significant overlap, generating a smaller and more focused number of codes. One then looks across these smaller pieces of data, comparing and contrasting how a particular explanatory framework fits or doesn't fit new situations and phenomena. According to Strauss and Corbin (1994), "In this methodology, theory may be *generated* initially from the data, or, if existing (grounded) theories seem appropriate to the area of investigation, then these may be *elaborated* and modified as incoming data are meticulously played against them" (p. 273). Perhaps an example might help. Looking across the interviews and fieldnotes from my research project on hip-hop, I saw the notion of place emerge as central. Even more specifically, notions of Southerness were drawn upon in several different contexts—talking about music, people, places, often in widely divergent ways. Grounded theory allowed me to see how this notion was used and not used in different ways across the data—for example, talking about personal respect and talking about community—in ways that were both complementary and distinct. I wound up arguing that notions of place allowed young people to draw together and live through certain situated notions of self and community in ways that were both unfolding and flexible.

The notion that one can build theory from data is an important one. Yet the language of coding often obscures the very personal and often idio-syncratic process of interpreting our data. As Laurel Richardson (1994) notes, many of our best insights emerge in the process of writing itself; that writing is a method of inquiry. Following Richardson, it is important to challenge the very simple notion that writing reflects ideas preformed or worked out in our minds. Instead, we understand our data in new ways in and through the writing process. Moreover, different writing genres give us access to differ-ent kinds of knowledges. The traditional research report privileges a linear approach to writing, one which privileges a set of extractable "findings" that speak back to a "hole" in the data. Other forms of writing privilege other kinds of knowledge—for example, ethnographic narratives often embed their insights in the narrative itself. We see this in texts such as Leif Gustavson's *Youth Learning on Their Own Terms* (2007), which follows the out-of-school creative practices (graffiti, slam poetry, and turntabling) of three youths over a year-long period. Many of Gustavson's most important findings are to be found in the deeply textured stories he tells about these youths. There is also a small but grow-ing body of work that privileges experimentation in writing—including ethnographic fiction, poetry, and plays. Each of these allows us to see our partici-pants and their actions in different kinds of ways. Richardson (1994) writes,

> Although we usually think of writing as a mode of "telling" about the social world, writing is not just a mopping-up activity at the end of a research project. Writing is also a way of "knowing"—a method of discovery and analysis. By writing in different ways, we discover new aspects of our topic and our relationship to it. Form and content are inseparable. (p. 516)

Emerson, Fretz, and Shaw (1995) underscore this point, noting that key themes often emerge in the writing process itself. As they write,

> In terms of writing, developing a thematic narra-tive requires constant movement back and forth

between specific fieldnote incidents and progressively more focused and precise analysis. To facilitate this process, we do not recommend beginning with a tentative thesis or working hypothesis. Instead, we urge the writer to hold off formulating an explicit thesis until the paper is finished, so that even in the process of writing, she will make discoveries about data and continue to balance her analytic insights with the demands of sticking close to indigenous views. (p. 171)

Although Emerson, Fretz, and Shaw discuss fieldnotes, they underscore an important point—how do we find our own interpretive "voice" amidst empirical material that can speak to us in many different ways? What is the role of authorial control?—a question particularly pressing when dealing with marginalized groups. Different people have dealt with this in different ways. It is a question that has implications (as noted above) for the fieldwork process as well as the writing process. For example, one faces ethical questions when transcribing quotes from interviews or when pulling out fieldnotes. Some authors choose to deeply contextualize the interview process—showing the complex back-and-forth between interviewer and interviewee, showing how the discussion itself perhaps shaped the response. Others will more explicitly pull out quotes and insert them into the ethnographic narrative. Some authors choose to present their fieldnotes in the text itself in somewhat "raw" form—evidencing the complex and often tentative social surround of any field-based observations. Others will simply paraphrase "what happened." There are no clear dictums about these approaches. Some would argue that the former approaches are more ethical as they give the subjects more autonomy in the text. Others argue that this is misleading, that the author is always in control and it is his or her responsibility to construct a powerful and compelling narrative about the topic in question.

New Methodological Presses

I have tended to stress throughout the interpretive nature of the research and writing process. Yet it is important to note that qualitative researchers today are under pressure to make their methods of collecting and interpreting data more visible, extractible, and in some ways replicable. We see this evidenced most clearly in the document "Standards on Reporting on Empirical Research in AERA Publication," published recently in *Educational Researcher* (American Educational Research Association, AERA, 2006). AERA is the central umbrella organization for the academic field of education. Although the discussion is most obviously germane to the tier-one journals it publishes, the implications are far-reaching for qualitative inquiry. The document outlines very specific requirements for reporting on empirical data—from problem formulation to design and logic, sources of evidence, measurement and classification, analysis and interpretation, generalization, and ethics in reporting. Although the document takes pains not to draw sharp splits between qualitative and quantitative work, it is quite clear that the implications for qualitative work are more far-ranging.

Most specifically, all the recommendations (and I encourage the reader to read it carefully) are undergirded by two main goals. The first is to make sure all claims in empirical research are explicitly warranted. That is, adequate evidence needs to be marshaled and presented in very explicit ways whenever a claim or conclusion is made, including a description of how it was collected and under what circumstances. Contrary evidence should also be made available. The second goal is to make sure all methodological discussions are entirely "transparent" (p. 33). That is, methodological decisions need to be justified and described every step of the way. As AERA notes, "Reporting should make explicit the logic of inquiry and activities that led from the development of the initial interest, topic, problem, or research question; through the definition, collection, and analysis of empirical evidence; to the articulated outcomes of the study" (p. 33). For example, AERA recommends that the coding process (discussed above) be justified and described in very concrete ways. They recommend including the background of the coders, having others cross-check the codes for reliability, and even having participants check the codes themselves (p. 36). By advocating these standards, the document seeks to make qualitative methods more visible, extractable, and ready to handle.

This methodological press will be with us all for the foreseeable future. As with most such presses, there is great possibility as well as danger here. On the one hand, the document seeks to set the ground for the wider circulation and dissemination of qualitative research findings. Reporting that takes these standards into account, according to the document, and "permits scholars to understand one another's work, prepares that work for public scrutiny, and enables others to use that work" (p. 33). Warranted and transparent scholarship can more readily be reproduced in other sites and settings, allowing for a broader conversation about the issues and concerns facing us all today—for example, poverty and its effects on youths around the world. At its most helpful, such a document works against the continued marginalization of qualitative work in the production and circulation of academic knowledge.

On the other hand, much qualitative work is, in fact, highly interpretive and personal, often bearing the particular imprint of the researcher. In qualitative research, the researcher "is" the research instrument. Our literal, embodied presence in the field—observing the social surroundings, participating in the flux and flow of human interaction, or interviewing participants—matters. Moreover, our texts very much bear our own literary voice and presence—a point made by James Clifford and George Marcus (1986) in the ways noted above. Making methods extractible in this fashion can potentially work to hide the researcher's presence in the study. At worst, it can allow the researcher to abdicate his or her particular responsibilities for the entire arc of the research process. Although these efforts to make qualitative research a seemingly more "precise science" contain risks as well as possibilities, they cannot be avoided. This is particularly true for those who look to publish in tier-one journals, acquire large grants, or secure jobs and tenure at Research 1 universities.

I turn now to another set of presses researchers must increasingly negotiate.

Institutional Review Boards

The ethical concerns discussed throughout this book have been largely intra- and interpersonal ones, negotiated in particular ways between researchers and researchers and their participants. A more formal set of ethical reviews and requirements are now legally institutionalized in **institutional review boards (IRBs)** or human subject review boards (HSRBs). These boards are housed, by federal law, at universities and colleges and are designed to protect the subjects of our work. Anyone conducting work with people (as opposed, for example, to publicly available documents or media texts) must get approval from these boards. Every college and university has documents outlining the process, typically available online.

As Clifford Christians (2005) and others have pointed out, these boards arose in response to egregious abuses in the biomedical field—a key example being the Tuskegee Syphilis Experiment, conducted between 1932 and 1972, where African American men infected with the disease were willfully deceived about their condition and not given proper treatment. In 1978, the U.S. National Commission for the Protection of Human Subjects in Biomedical and Behavioral Research was established. Three basic principles were established and published as the so-called Belmont Report (Christians, 2005, p. 146). First, researchers have to insure that human subjects enter research will-

Institutional review boards (IRBs)

housed, by federal law, at universities and colleges and designed to protect the human subjects of our work. Based on the principles of "respect," "beneficence," and "justice." In the end, such boards weigh the benefits and risks of research proposals and approve them or not accordingly.

ingly and with full knowledge of its risks and benefits. Minors and others with so-called diminished autonomy are afforded special protections here. This is often called the principle of respect. Second, researchers must avoid harming their subjects. This is often called the principle of beneficence. Third, researchers must distribute both the "benefits and burdens of research" fairly (p. 146). That is, marginalized groups cannot be overused or manipulated owing to their vulnerability. This is often called the principle of justice. In the end, the benefits of research must outweigh its risks.

These principles were put forward to address abuses of the past. But, as previously noted, many of these abuses happened in the biomedical realm. It is often difficult to translate these concerns to the particularities of qualitative research, where research relationships are often negotiated on the terrain of mutual respect between autonomous agents. (Of course, most of the classic ethnographic studies conducted before the 1980s did not have to deal with them.) In addition, as noted, the concept of "youth" does not translate easily across culture or class. A working-class 16-year-old responsible for the material maintenance and upkeep of a household is not the same as an affluent 16-year-old still largely locked into the in-between model of teenage life. Yet in this model they are. Indeed, IRBs often substitute a legal language for a truly ethical one. Personal relationships are reduced to contractually legal ones, as evidenced by the informed consent forms researchers are now compelled to use. Even the language of "human subjects" is an alienating one—one perhaps useful for large-scale medical experiments but not always for human relationships.

That being said, we should remember that IRBs are law now for a reason—researchers have abused their power in the past. Moreover, it is important to remember that IRBs are often the only source of protection truly disenfranchised youths have. Middle-class and elite parents, for example, can often effectively "police" the role of researchers in the lives of their children. This is one of the advantages of having power and cultural capital. It is also one of the reasons there is comparatively little research on elites. The same is not always the case for poor and marginalized youths. As noted throughout, this is a population often exploited by those with power. Imperfect as they are, IRBs can be a powerful source of protection here.

In sum, the dominant questions researchers face from IRBs are—what are the risks of this research? What are the benefits both to the participants and also to the general field of knowledge? And, finally, does this bargain make sense? IRBs must be approached in this spirit—and with full knowledge that they arose as a result of (sometimes deadly) academic abuses of the past.

Conclusion

I have attempted to unpack here some of the back-stage work that goes into the ethnographic endeavor. This chapter was not meant to offer concrete suggestions for conducting such work—I have tried to offer readers resources for further study—but to perhaps demystify what happens in the research process. Such an impulse is necessary, to return to the opening discussion, as so much work on urban youth culture has tended to calcify itself in delimiting ways. Prying open this discussion allows us to take the next step—to reengage urban youth culture with a new and expansive research imaginary. If nothing else, I hope this book is a contribution to this critically important endeavor.

GLOSSARY

Approaches—formations that provide loosely defined structures for conceiving, designing, and carrying out research projects. For example, does one do ethnography, life history, and/or grounded theory studies?

Epistemologies—concerned with the question of knowledge and how people come to possess it. For example, does one have an objectivist or interpretive understanding of the world?

Fieldnotes—the primary records researchers keep of their experiences in the field. Writing fieldnotes is a deeply interpretive endeavor. They reveal what we choose to focus on and our descriptions can often mirror our own biases. The best, most useful fieldnotes attempt to document in detail ongoing social action. They do not move too quickly to interpretation. They record detail—for example, who said what to whom and under (exactly) what circumstances. They do not describe scenes with generic phrases such as "chaotic." They describe what is happening. They do not describe people as character types, such as "controlling." They describe individual action in detail. They do not interpret broad, social processes too quickly with limited data.

Grounded theory—the impulse to build ground-up theories about social phenomena from extant data. Typically, this method entails "coding" one's data—first, open coding and, second, focused coding. One then looks across these smaller pieces of data, comparing and contrasting how a particular explanatory framework "fits" or doesn't "fit" new situations and phenomena. The result is a theory built from the data themselves.

Institutional review boards (IRBs)—or human subject review boards (HSRBs)—are housed, by federal law, at universities and colleges and are designed to protect the subjects of our work. Anyone conducting work with people (as opposed, for example, to publicly available documents or media texts) must get approval from these boards. In 1978, the U.S. National Commission for the Protection of Human Subjects in Biomedical and Behavioral Research was established. Three basic principles were established and published as the so-called Belmont Report—the principles of "respect," "beneficence," and "justice." In the end, such boards weigh the benefits and risks of research proposals and approve them or not accordingly.

Interviews—structured, semistructured, or unstructured conversations between researchers and research participants. They can be conducted with single individuals or can be larger group discussions or focus groups. Whereas participant-observation allows the researcher to understand how participants interact in a naturalistic context, interviews allow the researcher to understand more explicitly how participants understand their experiences. Interviews allow researchers to understand how individuals make sense out of their experiences—give them shape and nuance. They are a particularly good way to understand people's beliefs—or at least their articulated beliefs. Such interviews are typically tape recorded and transcribed.

Literature review—the section of a research report or book that describes how others have written about one's particular object of analysis. It should both demonstrate full competency in a particular domain of inquiry and show how one's work either fills a "gap" or extends an ongoing academic discussion.

Narratives—typically first-person stories people tell about particular incidents, events, and people. According to linguist William Labov (1972), a "fully formed narrative" has an abstract (which summarizes the story), an orientation (which introduces the parties, place, and time relevant to the story), at least one complicating action (what happened to mark these events as special), an evaluation (the way the speaker responded to the complicating action), a resolution (what finally happened), and a coda (which returns the speaker to the present) (pp. 362–396).

Participant-observation—method in which researchers spend long stretches of time with social actors in specific naturalistic contexts as a way to investigate, document, and experience ongoing social action. As opposed to formal interviews, this method allows the researcher to engage participants on unfamiliar terrain, fostering new kinds of understandings about how people give meaning to their lives, experiences, and events.

Research question—the overarching guiding question one has about a particular social phenomenon or body of theory or literature. Constructing such a question is both a deeply ethical and aesthetic undertaking. No such question is neutral or value free. Such a question should also script its own place into an ongoing academic discussion—its gaps as well as key areas of inquiry.

Strategies—methods or techniques used to collect and analyze empirical material. For example, does one use interviews, observations, or archival data?

Theories—abstract sets of assumptions and assertions used to interpret, understand, and act upon individual, social, and cultural processes and dynamics. For example, is one a Marxist, feminist, and/or poststructuralist?

References

American Educational Research Association. (2006). Standards for reporting on empirical social science research in AERA publication. *Educational Researcher,* 35(6), 33–40.

Anderson, E. (1990). *Streetwise: Race, class, and change in an urban community.* Chicago: University of Chicago Press.

Anderson, E. (1999). *Code of the street: Decency, violence, and the moral life of the inner city.* New York: W.W. Norton.

Appadurai, A. (1996). *Modernity at large: Cultural dimensions of globalization.* Minneapolis, MN: University of Minnesota Press.

Appadurai, A. (2006). The right to research. *Globalisation, Societies, and Education,* 4(2), 167–177.

Arnot, M. (2004). Male working-class identities and social justice. In N. Dolby, G. Dimitriadis, and P. Willis (Eds.). *Learning to labor in new times* (pp. 17–40). New York: Routledge.

Aron-Dine, A., and Shapiro, I. (2006). *New data show extraordinary jump in income concentration in 2004.* Center on Budget and Policy Priorities. Available at: http://www.cbpp.org/7–10–06inc.htm.

Atkinson, P., Coffey, A., and Delamont, S. (2003). *Key themes in qualitative research.* Walnut Creek, CA: Alta Mira Press.

Ball, A., and Heath, S. B. (1993). Dances of identity: Finding an ethnic self in the arts. In S.B. Heath and M. McLaughlin (Eds.), *Identity* and inner-city youth: Beyond ethnicity and gender (pp. 69–93). New York: Teachers College Press.

Bourdieu, P. (1984). *Distinction: A social critique of the judgment of taste* (R. Nice, Trans.). Cambridge, MA: Harvard University Press.

Bourgois, P. (1995). *In search of respect: Selling crack in el barrio.* Cambridge: Cambridge University Press.

Brotherton, D., and Barrios, L. (2004). *The almighty Latin king and queen nation.* New York: Columbia University Press.

Brunner, C., and Tally, W. (1999). *The new media literacy handbook: An educator's guide to bringing new media into the classroom.* New York: Doubleday.

Buckingham, D. (1993). *Children talking television: The making of television literacy.* London: The Falmer Press.

Buckingham, D. (1996). *Moving images: Understanding children's emotional responses to television.* Manchester: Manchester University Press.

Buckingham, D. (Ed.). (1998). *Teaching popular culture: Beyond radical pedagogy.* London: UCL Press.

Buckingham, D., and Sefton-Green, J. (1995). *Cultural studies goes to school: Reading and teaching popular media.* London: Taylor & Francis.

Bulmer, M. (1984). *The Chicago school of sociology: Institutionalization, diversity, and the rise of sociological research.* Chicago: University of Chicago Press.

Burawoy, M., Blum, J. A., George, S., et al. (2000). *Global ethnography.* Berkeley: University of California Press.

Burton, L., Obeidallah, D., and Allison, K. (1996). Ethnographic insights on social context and adolescent development among inner-city African-American teens. In R. Jessor, A. Colby, and R. Shweder (Eds.), *Ethnography and human development: Context and meaning in social inquiry* (pp. 395–418). Chicago: University of Chicago Press.

Cammarota, J., and Fine, M. (Eds.). (forthcoming). *Revolutionizing education: Youth participatory action research in education.* New York: Routledge.

Chang, J. (2005). *Can't stop, won't stop: A history of the hip-hop generation.* New York: St. Martin's Press.

Christians, C. (2005). Ethics and politics in qualitative research. In N. Denzin and Y. Lincoln (Eds.), *The handbook of qualitative research* (3rd ed.) (pp. 139–164). Thousand Oaks, CA: Sage.

Clarke, J., Hall, S., Jefferson, T., and Roberts, B. (1976). Subcultures, cultures, and class: A theoretical overview In S. Hall and T.

Jefferson (Eds.) *Resistance through rituals* (pp. 9–74). Birmingham, UK: Open University Press.

Clifford, J. (1997). *Routes.* Cambridge, MA: Harvard University Press.

Clifford, J., and Marcus, G. (Eds.). (1986). *Writing culture: The poetics and politics of ethnography.* Berkeley: University of California Press.

Condry, I. (2006). *Hip-hop Japan: Rap and the paths of cultural globalization.* Durham, NC: Duke University Press.

Cornbleth, C. (2003). *Hearing America's youth.* New York: Peter Lang.

Cross, G. (2004). *The cute and the cool: Wondrous innocence and modern American children's culture.* New York: Oxford University Press.

Dance, J. (2002). *Tough fronts: The impact of street culture on schooling.* New York: Routledge.

Denzin, N. (2002). *Reading race.* Thousand Oaks, CA: Sage.

Denzin, N., and Giardina, M. (Eds.). (2007). *Ethical futures in qualitative research.* Walnut Creek, CA: Left Coast Press.

Denzin, N., and Lincoln, Y. (2005). *Handbook of qualitative research* (3rd ed.). Thousand Oaks, CA: Sage.

Dimitriadis, G. (2001). *Performing identity/performing culture: Hip hop as text, pedagogy, and lived practice.* New York: Peter Lang.

Dimitriadis, G. (2003). *Friendship, cliques, and gangs: Young black men coming of age in urban America.* New York: Teachers College Press.

Dimitriadis, G., and McCarthy, C. (2001). *Reading and teaching the postcolonial: From Baldwin to Basquiat and Beyond.* New York: Teachers College Press.

Dimitriadis, G., and Weis, L. (2001). Imagining possibilities with and for contemporary youth: (Re)writing and (re)visioning education today. *Qualitative Research, 1*(2), 223–240.

Dolby, N. (2000). Changing selves: Multicultural education and the challenge of new identities. *Teachers College Record, 102*(5), 898–912.

Dolby, N. (2001). *Constructing race: Youth, identity, and popular culture in South Africa.* Albany: State University of New York Press.

Drake, S., and Cayton, H. (1945). *Black metropolis: A study of Negro life in a Northern city.* Chicago: University of Chicago Press.

Duneier, M. (1992). *Slim's table: Race, respectability, and masculinity.* Chicago: University of Chicago Press.

Eisenhart, M. (2001). Educational ethnography past, present, and future: Ideas to think with. *Educational Researcher, 30*(8), 16–27.

Eisenhart, M., and Finkel, E. (1998). *Women's science: Learning and succeeding from the margins.* Chicago: University of Chicago Press.

Emerson, R., Fretz, R., and Shaw, L. (1995). *Writing ethnographic fieldnotes.* Chicago: University of Chicago Press.

Faris, R. (1967). *Chicago sociology: 1920–1932.* Chicago: University of Chicago Press.

Fine, M. (1991). *Framing dropouts: Notes on the politics of an urban public high school.* Albany: State University of New York Press.

Fine, M. (1994). Working the hyphens: Reinventing self and other in qualitative research. In N. Denzin and Y. Lincoln (Eds.), *Handbook of qualitative research* (pp. 70–82). Thousand Oaks, CA: Sage.

Fine, M. (2004). *Echoes of Brown: Youth documenting and performing the legacy of* Brown v. Board of Education. New York: Teachers College Press.

Fine, M. (2006). Bearing witness: Methods for researching oppression and resistance. A textbook for critical research methods. *Social Justice Research, 19*(1), 83–108.

Fine, M., and Weis, L. (1998). *The unknown city: Lives of poor and working-class young adults.* Boston: Beacon Press.

Fine, M., Weis, L., Centrie, C., and Roberts, R. (2000). Educating beyond the borders of schooling. *Anthropology and Education Quarterly, 31*(2), 131–151.

Fine, M., Weis, L., Weseen, S., and Wong, L. (2000). For whom? Qualitative research, representations, and social responsibilities. In N. Denzin and Y. Lincoln (Eds.), *Handbook of qualitative research* (2nd Ed.) (pp. 107–131). Thousand Oaks, CA: Sage Publications.

Fleisher, M. (1998). *Dead end kids: Gang girls and the boys they know.* Milwaukee: University of Wisconsin Press.

Forman, M. (2002). *The 'hood comes first: Race, space, and place in rap and hip-hop.* Middletown, CT: Wesleyan University Press.

Forman, M., and Neal, M. (Eds.). (2004). *That's the joint! The hip-hop studies reader.* New York: Routledge.

Geertz, C. (1973). *The interpretation of cultures.* New York: Basic Books.

Gilmore, P., and Glatthorn, A. (Eds.). (1982). *Children in and out of school: Ethnography and education.* Washington, DC: Center for Applied Linguistics.

Ginwright, S., and Cammarota, J. (2006). Introduction. In S. Ginwright, P. Noguera, and J. Cammarota (Eds.), *Beyond resis-*

tance! Youth activism and community change (pp. xiii–xxii). New York: Routledge.

Giroux, H. (2004). *The terror of neoliberalism.* Boulder, CO: Paradigm Publishers.

Goodman, S. (2003). *Teaching youth media: A critical guide to literacy, video production and social change.* New York: Teachers College Press.

Grossberg, L. (2005). *Caught in the crossfire: Kids, politics, and America's future.* Boulder, CO: Paradigm Press.

Gustavson, L. (2007). *Youth learning on their own terms.* New York: Routledge.

Hall, J. (2001). *Canal town youth: Community organization and the development of adolescent identity.* Albany: State University of New York Press.

Hall, S., and Jefferson, T. (Eds.). (1976). *Resistance through rituals: Youth subcultures in post-war Britain.* Birmingham, UK: Open University Press.

Hannerz, U. (1969). *Soulside: Inquiries into ghetto culture and community.* New York: Columbia University Press.

Hannerz, U. (1980). *Exploring the city: Inquiries toward an urban anthropology.* New York: Columbia University Press.

Harris, A. (Ed.). (forthcoming). *Next wave cultures: Feminisms, subcultures, activism.* New York: Routledge.

Hart, C. (1999). *Doing a literature review: Releasing the social science research imagination.* Thousand Oaks, CA: Sage.

Head, S. (2003). *The new ruthless economy : Work & power in the digital age.* New York: Oxford University Press.

Heath, S. B. (1983). *Ways with words: Language, life, and work in communities and classrooms.* Cambridge: Cambridge University Press.

Heath, S. B. (1991). Inner-city life to literature: Drama in language learning. *TESOL Quarterly, 27*(2), 177–192.

Heath, S. B. (1996). Ruling places: Adaptation in development by inner-city youth. In R. Jessor, A. Colby, and R. Schweder (Eds.), *Ethnography and human development: Context and meaning in social inquiry* (pp. 225–251). Chicago: University of Chicago Press.

Heath, S. B. (2001). Three's not a crowd: Plans, roles, and focus in the arts. *Educational Researcher, 30*(7), 10–17.

Heath, S. B., and McLaughlin, M (Eds.). (1993). *Identity and inner-city youth: Beyond ethnicity and gender.* New York: Teachers College Press.

Heath, S. B., and McLaughlin, M. (1994). The best of both worlds: Connecting community schools and community youth organizations for all-day, all-year learning. *Educational Administration Quarterly, 30*(3), 278–300.

Hebdige, D. (1979). *Subculture: The meaning of style.* London: Routledge.

Helfenbein, R. (2006). Thinking through scale: Critical geography and curriculum spaces. Unpublished paper presented at the "Articulating the Present (Next) Moment in Curriculum Studies" conference, Purdue University, February 16–19.

Hill, A. (Ed.). (forthcoming). *Next wave cultures: Feminism, subcultures, activism.* New York: Routledge.

Holstein, J., and Gubrium, J. (Eds.). (2003). *Inside interviewing: New lenses, new concerns.* Thousand Oaks, CA: Sage.

Huq, R. (2006). *Beyond subculture: Pop, youth and identity in a postcolonial world.* New York: Routledge.

Institute for Local Governance and Regional Growth, University at Buffalo. (2006). *Poverty in New York State and Buffalo Niagara: Updates from the U.S. Census Bureau.* Available at: http://www.regional-institute.buffalo.edu/includes/UserDownloads/Oct06_Poverty.pdf

Jackson, J. (2001). *Harlemworld: Doing race and class in contemporary black America.* Chicago: University of Chicago Press.

James, C., and Saul, R. (forthcoming) Urban schooling in suburban context: Exploring the immigrant factor in urban education. In W. Pink. (Ed.), *International Handbook of Urban Education.* Westport, CT: Greenwood Press.

Jenkins, H. (2006). *Convergence culture: Where old and new media collide.* New York: NYU Press.

Kamberelis, G., and Dimitriadis, G. (2005). *On qualitative inquiry.* New York: Teachers College Press.

Katz, C. (1999). Disintegrating developments: Global economic restructuring and the eroding ecologies of youth. In T. Skelton and G. Valentine (Eds.), *Cool Places: Geographies of Youth Cultures* (pp. 130–144). London and New York: Routledge.

Katz, C. (2001). On the grounds of globalization: A topography for feminist political engagements. *Signs, 26*(4), 1213–1237.

Kelley, G. (1997). *From Vietnam to America: A chronicle of the Vietnamese immigration of the United States.* Boulder, CO: Westview Press.

Kincheloe, J. (1998). The new childhood: Home alone as a way of life. In H. Jenkins (Ed.), *The children's culture reader* (pp. 159–177). New York: NYU Press.

Kitwana, B. (2005). *Why white kids love hip hop.* New York: Basic Books.

Kotkin, J. (2006). *The city: A global history.* New York: The Modern Library.

Labov, W. (1972). *Language in the inner city: Studies in the black English vernacular.* Philadelphia: University of Pennsylvania Press.

Lashua, B. (2005). Making music, re-making leisure in the beat of Boyle Street. Unpublished Ph.D. dissertation, University of Alberta, Canada.

Levinson, B., and Holland, D. (1996). The cultural production of the educated person: An introduction. In B. Levinson, Foley, D., and Holland, D. (Eds.). *The cultural production of the educated person: Critical ethnographies of schooling and local practices* (pp. 1–31). Albany: State University of New York Press.

Liebow, E. (1967/2003). *Tally's corner: A study of Negro streetcorner men.* Lanham, MD: Rowman & Littlefield.

MacLeod, J. (1995). *Ain't no making it: Aspirations and attainment in a low-income neighborhood.* Boulder, CO: Westview Press.

Madriz, E. (2000). Focus groups in feminist research. In N. Denzin and Y. Lincoln (Eds.), *Handbook of qualitative research* (2nd ed.) (pp. 835–850). Thousand Oaks, CA: Sage.

Mahiri, J. (1998). *Shooting for excellence: African American and youth culture in new century schools.* Urbana, IL: National Counsel of Teachers of Education.

Males, M. (1996). *The scapegoat generation: America's war on adolescence.* Monroe, ME: Common Courage Press.

Marcus, G. (1986). Contemporary problems of ethnography in the modern world system. In J. Clifford and G. Marcus (Eds.), *Writing culture: The poetics and politics of ethnography* (pp. 165–193). Berkeley: University of California Press.

Marcus, G. (1998). *Ethnography through thick and thin.* Princeton: Princeton University Press.

Marshall, C., and Rossman, G. (1995). The substance of the study: Framing the research question. In *Designing qualitative research* (pp. 15–37). Thousand Oaks, CA: Sage.

Massey, D. (1994) *Space, place, and gender.* Minneapolis: University of Minneapolis Press.

McCarthy, C. (1998). *The uses of culture: Education and the limits of ethnic affiliation.* New York: Routledge.

McCarthy, C. et al. (Eds.). (2008). *Globalizing cultural studies: Ethnographic interventions in theory, method and policy.* New York: Peter Lang.

McCormick, J. (2004). *Writing in the asylum: Student poets in city schools.* New York: Teachers College Press.

McLaren, P. (1997). *Revolutionary multiculturalism: Pedagogies of dissent for the new millennium.* Boulder, CO: Westview Press.

McLaughlin, M., and Irby, M. (1994). Urban sanctuaries: Neighborhood organizations that keep hope alive. *Phi Delta Kappan, 76*(4), 300–304.

McLaughlin, M., Irby, M., and Langman, J. (1994). *Urban sanctuaries: Neighborhood organizations in the lives and futures of inner-city youth.* San Francisco: Jossey-Bass Publishers.

McRobbie, A. (1991). *Feminism and youth culture: From* Jackie *to* Just Seventeen. Boston: Unwin Hyman.

Mitchell, T. (Ed.). (2001). *Global noise: Rap and hip-hop outside the USA.* Middletown, CT: Wesleyan University Press.

Nespor, J. (1997). *Tangled up in school: Politics, space, bodies, and signs in the educational process (sociocultural, political, and historical studies in education).* Mahwah, NJ: Lawrence Erlbaum Associates.

Nightingale, C. (1995). *On the edge: A history of poor black children and their dreams.* New York: Basic Books.

Nolan, K. (2007). Disciplining Urban Youth: An Ethnographic Study of a Bronx High School. Unpublished Ph.D. dissertation, CUNY Graduate Center, New York.

Nolan, K., and Anyon, J. (2004). Learning to do time. In N. Dolby, G. Dimitriadis, and P. Willis (Eds.), *Learning to labor in new times* (pp. 133–149). New York: Routledge.

Orfield, M. (2002). *American metropolitics: The new suburban reality.* Washington, DC: Brookings Institute.

Ortner, S. (Ed.). (1999). *The Fate of "culture": Geertz and beyond.* Berkeley: University of California Press.

Park, R. (1925). The city: Suggestions for the investigation of human behavior in the urban environment; The growth of the city: An introduction to a research project. In R. Park and E. Burgess (Eds.), *The city: An investigation of human behavior in the urban environment* (pp. 1–61). Chicago: University of Chicago Press.

Poland, B. (2003). Transcription quality. In J. Holstein and J. Gubrium (Eds.), *Inside interviewing: New lenses, new concerns* (pp. 267–288). Thousand Oaks, CA: Sage.

Reich, R. B. (1991). *The work of nations: Preparing ourselves for 21st century capitalism.* New York: A.A. Knopf.

Reich, R. B. (2001). *The future of success.* New York: A.A. Knopf.

Richardson, L. (1994). Writing: A method of inquiry. In N. Denzin and Y. Lincoln (Eds.). *Handbook of qualitative research* (pp. 516–529). Thousand Oaks, CA: Sage.

Riessman, C. (1993). *Narrative analysis.* Newbury Park, CA: Sage.

Rosaldo, R. (1990). *Culture and truth.* Boston: Beacon Press.

Rose, T. (1994). *Black noise.* Hanover: Wesleyan University Press.

Said, E. (2003/1978). *Orientalism.* New York: Vintage Books.

Sassen, S. (2003). The impact of new technologies on globalization in cities. In R. Legates and F. Stout (Eds.), *The city reader* (3rd ed.) (pp. 212–220). New York: Routledge.

Seidman, I. (2006). *Interviewing as qualitative research.* New York: Teachers College Press.

Sefton-Green, J. (Ed.). (1998). *Digital diversions: Youth culture in the age of multimedia.* New York: Routledge.

Sefton-Green, J. (Ed.). (1999). *Young people, creativity and new technologies.* New York: Routledge.

Smith, Z. (2000). *White teeth.* New York: Random House.

Spindler, G. (Ed.). (2000). *Fifty years of anthropology and education: 1950–2000.* Mahwah, NJ: Lawrence Erlbaum Associates.

Spring, J. (1989). The sorting machine revisited: National educational policy since 1945. New York: Longman.

Stack, C. (1974). *All our kin: Strategies for survival in a black community.* New York: Harper Torchbook.

Steinberg, S., and Kincheloe, J. (2004). *Kinderculture: The corporate construction of childhood.* Cambridge, MA: Westview Press.

Strauss, A., and Corbin, J. (1994). Grounded theory methodology: An overview. In N. Denzin and Y. Lincoln (Eds.), *Handbook of qualitative research* (pp. 262–272). Thousand Oaks, CA: Sage.

Sylvan, R. (2005). *Trance formation: The spiritual and religious dimensions of global rave culture.* New York: Routledge.

Templeton, I. (2006). What's so German about it? Race and cultural identity in Berlin's hip hop community. Unpublished Ph.D. dissertation, University of Stirling, Scotland.

Thornberry, T. (1998). Membership in youth gangs and involvement in serious and violent offending. In R. Loeber & D. Farrington. Eds. *Serious and violent offenders: Risk factors and successful interventions* (pp. 147–166). Thousand Oaks, CA: Sage.

Thrasher, F. (1926). The gang as a symptom of community disorganization. *Journal of Applied Sociology, 1*(1), 3–27.

Thrasher, F. (1927). *The gang: A study of 1,316 gangs in Chicago.* Chicago: University of Chicago Press.

Tobin, J. (2000). *"Good guys don't wear hats": Children's talk about the media.* New York: Teachers College Press.

Tuck, E., and Fine, M. (2007). Inner angles: A range of ethical responses to/with indigenous/decolonizing theories. In N. Denzin and M.

Giardina. (Eds.), *Ethical futures in qualitative research: Decolonizing the politics of knowledge* (pp. 145–168). Walnut Creek, CA: Left Coast Press.

Vargas, J. (2006). *Catching hell in the city of angels: Life and meanings of blackness in South Central Los Angeles.* Minneapolis: University of Minnesota Press.

Venkatesh, S. (2003). A note on social theory and the American street gang. In L. Kontos, D. Brotherton, and L. Barrios (Eds.), *Gangs and society: Alternative perspectives* (pp. 3–11). New York: Columbia University Press.

Vidich, A., and Lyman, S. (2000). Qualitative methods: Their history in sociology and education. In N. Denzin and Y. Lincoln (Eds.), *Handbook of qualitative research* (2nd ed.) (pp. 37–84). Thousand Oaks, CA: Sage.

Wallace, C. (1987). *For richer, for poorer.* New York: Tavistock.

Weiler, J. (2000). *Codes and contradictions: Race, gender identity, and schooling.* Albany: State University of New York Press.

Weis, L., and Dimitriadis, G. (forthcoming). Dueling banjos: Shifting economic and cultural contexts in the lives of youth. *Teachers College Record.*

Weis, L., and Fine, M. (Eds.). (2000). *Construction sites: Excavating race, class, and gender among urban youth.* New York: Teachers College Press.

Weis, L., and Fine, M. (2001). Extraordinary conversations in public schools. *International Journal of Qualitative Studies in Education,* 14(4), 497–524.

Wertham, F. (1954). *Seduction of the innocent.* New York: Rinehart.

Whyte, W. F. (1943/1993). *Street corner society: The social structure of an Italian slum.* Chicago: University of Chicago Press.

Williams, R. (1961). *The long revolution.* London: Chatto & Windus.

Willis, P. (1977). *Learning to labor: How working class kids get working class jobs.* New York: Columbia University Press.

Willis, P. (1990). *Common culture: Symbolic work at play in everyday cultures of the young.* Milton Keynes, UK: Open University Press.

Wilson, W. (1996). *When work disappears: The world of the new urban poor.* New York: Vintage Books.

Wyn, J., and White, R. (1997). *Rethinking youth.* Thousand Oaks, CA: Sage.

Yon, D. (2000). *Elusive culture: Schooling, race, and identity in global times.* Albany: SUNY Press.

in Education

Peter Lang Primers are designed to provide a brief and concise introduction or supplement to specific topics in education. Although sophisticated in content, these primers are written in an accessible style, making them perfect for undergraduate and graduate classroom use. Each volume includes a glossary of key terms and a References and Resources section.

Other published and forthcoming volumes cover such topics as:

- Standards
- Popular Culture
- Critical Pedagogy
- Literacy
- Higher Education
- John Dewey
- Feminist Theory and Education

- Studying Urban Youth Culture
- Multiculturalism through Postformalism
- Creative Problem Solving
- Teaching the Holocaust
- Piaget and Education
- Deleuze and Education
- Foucault and Education

Look for more Peter Lang Primers to be published soon. To order other volumes, please contact our Customer Service Department:

800-770-LANG (within the US)
212-647-7706 (outside the US)
212-647-7707 (fax)

To find out more about this and other Peter Lang book series, or to browse a full list of education titles, please visit our website:
www.peterlang.com